Small Talk for Smart People

How Backwards Thinking Leads to Backwards Talking — and What I'm Learning to Do About It

Shawn M. Risner

About the Author

Shawn Risner is a loving husband and father, learning in real time how anchored thinking leads to clearer conversations. He writes from lived experience, not mastery, exploring how restraint, presence, and intention transform everyday interactions at home, at work, and in leadership.

Dedication

To my family,
for your patience, your grace, and your love
while I'm still learning in real time.

This book exists because you stayed
when I was still becoming.

Acknowledgements

This is to everyone who has impacted my life in one way or another.

To my amazing wife and best friend, Stephanie Risner, through God's grace, I have learned so much through you. I can't thank you enough. I can't thank God enough. You have been both my mirror and my anchor, even when the reflection wasn't easy to face.

To my incredible, beautiful children, Kennedy, Lance, Heaven, Lekhi, and Our Shia, I am beyond blessed with such rare and priceless souls. Each of you has taught me something different about patience, restraint, humility, and love. You have shaped me more than you will ever know.

To my parents, Sam Baker and Debbie Dotson, and Pastor Steve and Gilberta Henderson, thank you each for your roles and inspiration in my life. Your guidance, prayers, and example laid foundations long before I understood their value.

To my grandmother, Bernice Risner, words can never convey how thankful I am for you, for your love and sacrifice. I know you're up there in heaven cracking your jokes. I love you.

To all my siblings, on my father's side and my wife's side, the Hendersons, thank you for always being there.

To my fellow employee-owners at Roush Honda for a decade together. The lessons. The love. Priceless.

And to my brother, Bryan, my rock, you and I have been through it all from day one. You are truly one of my best friends.

Small Talk for Smart People
by Shawn M. Risner

Published by Rise Five LLC
Columbus, Ohio, USA
ISBN: 979-8-234-01564-8
Printed in the United States of America
First Edition
Cover design by Shawn M. Risner and Stephanie Risner

Disclaimer

This book is intended for informational and inspirational purposes only. The views and opinions expressed are those of the author and are not intended as professional, legal, psychological, or financial advice. Readers are responsible for how they apply the concepts presented thoughtfully and responsibly.

Scripture quotations are taken from the Holy Bible. Unless otherwise noted, all emphasis added is the author.

How Backwards Thinking Leads to Backwards Talking — and What I'm Learning to Do About It

Table of Contents

BREADCRUMBS

(A Foreword)

God woke me up at 4:30 in the morning.

I didn't get up right away. That's the honest part. He nudged. Then He nudged again. I finally got up and went downstairs, not knowing why, not planning to do anything. And then it came. Everything came. Every mistake I made. Every bad decision. Every moment I missed that I didn't even know mattered. It all came out. That's when I understood why He woke me up. God had been trying to get me to that moment for a long time. I just kept sleeping through it.

That's what breadcrumbs are. They're God nudging you, in a conversation you left unresolved, in something you said that you knew the moment it left your mouth wasn't right, in a room you misread, in a look from someone who loves you that you told yourself meant nothing. He lays them down. But looking down and picking them up, that part is yours. God won't do it for you. That's free will.

And the enemy knows that. John 10:10 says he comes to steal, kill, and destroy. And when he can't do that, he goes for the breadcrumbs. He uses wind. He scatters the trail. He fills your life with noise, distraction, and urgency, because he knows if the wind blows hard enough and long enough, you stop looking down. And a distracted man to the enemy is as good as a destroyed one. That's what he settled for with me.

I was distracted. I wasn't listening. God was using my wife to show me exactly where I was missing it. The things she tried to show me. The patience she carried while I kept walking past it. God was in all of that. She wasn't even a breadcrumb. She was a whole loaf of bread. I just wasn't paying attention.

So God changed His approach. He woke me up at 4:30 in the morning and sent me downstairs.

This book didn't start with a writing plan. It started as reflection notes. And somewhere in that process, it became something else entirely. It became repentance.

And you, the one holding this right now, this book in your hands is a breadcrumb too. The enemy has been busy. But God is persistent. And if He led you to this page, maybe this is your 4:30.

— Shawn

Before You Begin

This isn't a book about small talk.

I know what the title sounds like. Networking tips. Working a room. Making chitchat less painful.

That's not this.

This book is about the small moments hiding inside every conversation you have. The pause before you speak. The first five seconds of your response. The silence you don't fill, because you're too busy filling it.

I called it small talk because that's still my mistake. Not "used to be." Still. I've mastered nothing.

For a long time, I thought the moments that mattered were the big ones. The confrontations. The arguments. The talks you rehearse in the shower before you ever have them.

They weren't.

The moments that decided everything were smaller than that.

And I almost missed every one of them.

Chapter One

Anchored Thinking Comes First

"Let every person be quick to hear, slow to speak, slow to anger."

James 1:19

This isn't about silence.

It's about order.

For a long time, I believed I was at least a decent communicator.

Not exceptional. Not polished. But decent enough. I was willing to talk. Willing to engage. Willing to address things instead of avoiding them. And because I didn't shy away from conversations, especially difficult ones, I assumed that meant I was doing something right.

That assumption felt earned at the time.

I wasn't silent. I wasn't passive. I wasn't disappearing when things got uncomfortable. I showed up. I leaned in. I spoke my mind. And in my own internal scorecard, that counted for something.

Looking back, that assumption cost me more than I realized.

At the time, I thought conversations went wrong because the topic was difficult, the timing was off, or the other person simply misunderstood me. That explanation felt safe. It allowed me to move on without slowing down long enough to look at myself. Some conversations were just hard, I told myself. Some moments were poorly timed. Some people were more sensitive than others.

On the surface, that logic made sense.

But over time, it stopped holding up.

Because too many conversations followed the same pattern.

I would walk into a moment with good intentions. I wasn't angry. I wasn't trying to start a fight. I genuinely believed I was calm and composed. I told myself I was entering the conversation to make things better, not worse. And yet, by the time the conversation ended, the room often felt upside down, completely different than when I walked in.

The atmosphere changed. The tone shifted. Something invisible but undeniable happened.

I could feel it before I could name it. In my chest. In my shoulders. In the quiet that followed when neither of us quite knew what to say next. The conversation hadn't exploded, but it hadn't come together either. It just fractured.

I would leave those moments unsettled, replaying the conversation in my head, walking it backwards sentence by sentence, trying to find the exact point where things went sideways. I wasn't trying to win an argument. I was trying to understand how something that felt so reasonable in my head could come across so differently in real life.

I knew what I meant. I knew my intention. I could even explain, very clearly, what I was trying to communicate.

But intention alone didn't seem to matter.

What came across wasn't what I meant.

Slowly, and honestly, reluctantly, I began to realize something uncomfortable: conversations don't usually break down because of the words themselves. They break down because the thinking behind the words wasn't anchored before the words were spoken. I call this backwards thinking.

When thinking isn't anchored, talking becomes reactive, even when the tone sounds calm, even when the intention is good. The reaction doesn't always show up as anger. Sometimes it shows up as urgency. As explanation. As over-clarifying. As the subtle need to get your point across right now before something gets lost.

Backwards thinking doesn't always feel reckless in the moment. In fact, it often feels responsible. Necessary. Justified.

It shows up when the need to be understood takes over. When anxiety speeds up our responses. When we feel pressure to clarify before fully listening.

Instead of clarity guiding the conversation, emotion does. And emotion, when it isn't anchored, quietly hijacks direction.

I began to notice how often I entered conversations already leaning forward internally. My body was present, but my mind was racing ahead. I was forming responses while the other person was still speaking. I wasn't disengaged, I was over-engaged in the wrong direction.

I was listening to respond, not listening to understand.

This realization reframed everything.

That's backwards thinking.

And backwards thinking leads to backwards talking.

One moment at home made this painfully clear.

I remember sitting in a conversation with my wife where, just a few words in, I felt that familiar urge rise up, the need to jump in, clarify, explain, make sure my point was heard before anything went sideways. My jaw tightened. My thoughts started racing ahead of her words. I could feel myself preparing a response to something she hadn't even finished saying.

In the past, I would have jumped in immediately. I would have interrupted with good intentions and poor timing. And if I'm honest, most of the time when I did that, the conversation derailed fast.

She would become upset, not because she misunderstood my heart, but because she was responding to what I actually said. And that wasn't her fault. It was mine. My tone didn't match my intention. My words weren't anchored. Four or five words in, the conversation was already off track.

I would end up backpedaling. Explaining. Defending. Trying to clean up something I never meant to create in the first place. The more I explained, the more it sounded like excuses instead of responsibility.

That night, something different happened.

I paused.

Not because I suddenly mastered self-control. Not because I became wise overnight. I paused because something in me recognized the pattern. I could feel the old instinct rising, and for once, I didn't obey it.

I told myself, just hear her out. Completely.

So, I did.

And as she continued, something became clear, and uncomfortable. The point I was about to make, the one that felt so urgent and necessary, had almost nothing to do with what she was actually trying to say.

If I had interrupted, I wouldn't have clarified anything. I would have derailed the conversation entirely.

I would have responded to something she hadn't even finished expressing.

That moment exposed something I had to face how often I wasn't responding to reality. I was responding to my anticipation of my reality. I was reacting to what I thought was coming instead of what was actually being said.

That's backwards thinking.

And it doesn't just affect words. It affects tone. Body language. Facial expressions. Presence. Even silence.

I began to see how often my urgency was rooted in fear, fear of being misunderstood, fear of being blamed, fear of losing ground in the conversation before I even knew where it was going.

And instead of letting those fears settle, I let them drive my words.

When protection of self leads a conversation, it always costs connection.

I also began to recognize how often I entered conversations already braced. Not angry, but guarded. Ready. My body language reflected it before my words ever did. My shoulders were tense. My breathing shallow. My posture slightly forward, as if preparing for impact.

Even when my words were heard, my presence wasn't.

And here's the part that took the longest to admit many of the conversations that went wrong didn't go wrong because the other person was unreasonable. They went wrong because I hadn't settled myself before speaking.

Anchoring my thinking required something I wasn't used to doing, slowing down internally even when everything in me wanted to speed up.

It meant accepting that I didn't have to respond immediately. That silence didn't mean weakness. That pausing didn't mean losing ground.

I am learning that silence isn't absence. It's position.

When my thinking is anchored, silence becomes a tool instead of a threat. Pausing no longer feels like I'm giving something up. It feels like I'm gaining clarity.

That shift didn't happen overnight. It's still happening.

What anchoring has shown me is this: conversations don't need to be controlled to be effective. They need to be entered with intention. When my thinking is anchored, I don't feel the same pressure to prove, explain, or defend. I can let the conversation unfold instead of trying to steer it prematurely.

Anchored thinking doesn't eliminate disagreement. It eliminates unnecessary damage.

Once I began practicing anchoring, even imperfectly, I noticed something unexpected. Conversations felt less exhausting. I wasn't replaying them for hours afterward. I wasn't wishing I could take words back. I wasn't cleaning up my language nearly as often.

Not because I suddenly got everything right, but because I entered the conversation grounded.

Anchoring didn't make me passive. It made me precise.

It also helped me recognize something else: how often I confused being engaged with being effective. I thought that jumping in quickly showed care. I thought explaining immediately showed responsibility. I thought clarifying early showed leadership.

But leadership without anchoring isn't leadership. It's meaningless motion.

Anchored thinking creates alignment before expression. It gives your words weight because they aren't rushed. It gives your tone credibility because it isn't reactive. It gives your presence authority because it isn't anxious.

And when that happens, something subtle but powerful shifts: people feel safer talking to you. They don't brace. They don't guard. They don't rush to defend themselves before you even respond.

They finish their thoughts.

That alone changes everything.

Anchored thinking doesn't make conversations boring. It gives them depth.

Depth doesn't come from having more to say. It comes from saying what actually belongs.

That's the difference between speaking to be heard and speaking to be understood.

And it's the difference between backwards talking and intentional communication.

Application Layer, Chapter One

Anchored thinking is not a personality trait. It's a discipline.

Most conversations don't go wrong because people are careless. They go wrong because people are moving too fast internally. The mouth is responding, but the mind hasn't settled. The body is present, but the heart isn't.

Anchored thinking begins before the conversation starts.

Before you speak, slow yourself down enough to ask:
What am I feeling right now?
Am I anxious, rushed, defensive, or calm?
Do I feel the need to be heard immediately?
Am I entering this moment to understand, or to protect myself?

One of the most practical things I've learned is this: if I don't check my internal state first, my words will do the checking for me, and they won't do it gently.

Anchoring often looks like restraint:
Taking one intentional breath before responding
Letting the other person finish completely
Allowing silence to exist without filling it
Choosing clarity over urgency
Choosing presence over performance

Anchoring doesn't remove emotion. It regulates it.

Anchoring Scripture

"Let every person be quick to hear, slow to speak, slow to anger."

James 1:19

Reflection Prompts, Chapter One

What do I usually feel in my body before I speak in tense conversations?

How quickly do I move to suggest solutions when I feel misunderstood?

Where do I confuse urgency with clarity?

What does anchored thinking look like for me in real situations?

Which conversations in my life would change if I slowed down first?

Opportunity, Chapter One

Anchored thinking creates space.

Space for understanding.
Space for connection.
Space for words to reach people the way they were intended.

When your thinking is anchored:
You say fewer things you regret
You explain yourself less
You become safer to talk to

Anchored thinking doesn't make conversations shallow. It gives them weight.

And weight is what makes words matter. And anchored words create anchored relationships.

Chapter Two

The Illusion of Being Resolution-Based

"The purposes of a person's heart are deep waters,

but one who has insight draws them out."

Proverbs 20:5

Resolution requires depth before direction

For a long time, I told myself I was resolution-based.

That was the language I used, both internally and out loud. I wasn't emotional, I said. I was practical. I wasn't reactive. I was proactive. I wasn't defensive. I was just explaining my side. I wasn't trying to argue. I was trying to fix things.

At least, that's what I believed.

On the surface, that belief made sense. I valued solutions. I wanted problems resolved quickly. I didn't like loose ends. I didn't enjoy tension. I didn't want conversations dragging on longer than they needed to. To me, being resolution-based meant being mature, responsible, and forward-thinking.

I wore it like a badge.

But over time, something didn't add up.

Because despite my best intentions, many of those "solution-oriented" conversations didn't feel resolved at all. In fact, they often ended with more distance than clarity, more frustration than peace, more explaining than understanding.

I started noticing a pattern I couldn't ignore. The moment a difficult conversation began, my mind jumped ahead to the outcome.

How do we fix this? How do we get past this? How do we resolve this so we can move on?

Without realizing it, that forward jump caused me to skip something essential: actually, understanding what the problem was.

I thought I was being resolution-based. In reality, I was being outcome-obsessed.

There's a difference.

True resolution begins with understanding. But when your thinking isn't anchored, "resolution" becomes a shortcut, a way to bypass discomfort instead of working through it. And when that happens, the problem quietly shifts.

The disagreement becomes the issue instead of the root of it. The emotion becomes the obstacle instead of the signal. The other person becomes the problem instead of the situation you're both facing.

I didn't see that at first.

What I saw was inefficiency, delays, emotional detours. I wanted to get to the point. I wanted to fix the thing and move forward. And when someone slowed the conversation down with feelings, context, or perspective, it felt unnecessary, sometimes even frustrating.

But what I was missing was this: resolution doesn't come from speed. It comes from alignment.

And alignment can't happen if you're trying to fix something you haven't fully heard.

I began to realize that many of my "solutions" were actually me going completely based on assumption without hearing the other person. I wasn't offering clarity, I was redirecting the conversation before it finished forming. I wasn't solving the problem, I was redefining it based on my own assumptions.

That's not resolution. That's control.

And control, even when it sounds calm, has a way of shutting people down.

I saw this not just at home, but in everyday life.

There were moments at work when a colleague would bring an issue to me, and almost immediately I would shift into fix-it mode. I thought I was being helpful. I thought I was being efficient. I thought I was saving time.

But what I was really doing was skipping over something important: understanding their perspective.

I wasn't asking questions. I wasn't clarifying context. I wasn't slowing down enough to see the full picture.

I was solving my version of the problem, not their experience of it.

And when my solution didn't work, I felt confused.

Why isn't this helping? Why are they pushing back? Why does this still feel unresolved?

The answer was uncomfortable but simple.

I had made the person the problem.

Not intentionally. Not maliciously. But functionally.

When someone didn't respond well to my solution, I labeled them as resistant. When they needed more time, I labeled them as avoidant. When they didn't see things the way I did, I labeled them as emotional or irrational.

Those labels were just a defense mechanism.

They protected me from having to admit that I hadn't actually listened well enough to understand what was being asked of me.

Resolution-based thinking, when unanchored, has a blind spot: it assumes the problem is already clear.

But many conversations don't break down because people disagree on solutions. They break down because people never agreed on what the problem actually was.

I began to notice how often my urgency to fix it was rooted in discomfort rather than clarity.

I didn't like sitting in unresolved tension. I didn't like uncertainty. I didn't like conversations that felt open-ended. And instead of naming that discomfort, I tried to solve my way out of it.

Fixing became a coping mechanism.

If I could resolve the conversation quickly, I wouldn't have to sit with the emotions underneath it. I wouldn't have to face uncertainty. I wouldn't have to stay present in something that felt messy or unresolved.

But conversations aren't mechanical.

You can't tighten a bolt and move on. You can't patch over emotion with logic. You can't shortcut understanding.

The more I tried to fix things prematurely, the more I unintentionally shut people down.

And when people shut down, resolution becomes impossible.

I saw this clearly in moments with my wife.

She would begin sharing something that was weighing on her, and before she finished, my mind was already assembling a response. I thought I was helping. I thought I was being supportive. I thought I was preventing the conversation from spiraling.

But what I was really doing was signaling something else entirely: I've already decided what matters here.

She would respond, not to my intention, but to my words. And those words often hit like corrections instead of care, solutions instead of support, explanations instead of empathy.

Then I would feel misunderstood.

And here's where the illusion deepened.

When I felt misunderstood, I didn't slow down, I sped up. I explained more. Clarified more. Justified more. I doubled down on being "resolution-based," thinking that if I could just explain myself clearly enough, everything would click.

But clarity that arrives too early rarely feels like clarity. It feels like dismissal.

I had to confront something uncomfortable: I wasn't entering conversations to solve problems. I was entering them to end them.

I wanted the discomfort gone. The tension resolved. The moment wrapped up neatly.

But conversations don't work that way, at least not the important ones.

What I'm learning, slowly and not without resistance, is that not every conversation needs fixing. Some conversations need space. Some need listening. Some need time. And some need the freedom to unfold without being rushed toward an outcome.

Resolution-based thinking, when unanchored, becomes a way to avoid sitting with discomfort. It prioritizes ending the conversation over honoring it, and in doing so, it often creates the very tension it's trying to eliminate.

I also began to notice how often my need to "resolve" things was really a need to protect myself.

To protect myself from feeling inadequate. From uncertainty. From the discomfort of not having an answer right away.

And once I saw that, I couldn't unsee it.

Resolution had become a shield.

It allowed me to stay active in the conversation without being vulnerable. I could stay logical instead of empathetic, in control instead of present. I could talk at the problem instead of sitting with the person.

But control is not the same as leadership.

Leadership requires the ability to tolerate discomfort long enough for clarity to emerge.

That realization changed how I approached conversations. Instead of entering them with a solution already in mind, I began entering them with a question:

What is actually being asked of me here?

Sometimes the answer was obvious. Sometimes it wasn't. And sometimes, it surprised me.

There were moments when the person wasn't asking for advice at all. They weren't looking for a fix. They weren't asking me to solve anything. They simply needed to be heard. They needed space to process out loud. They needed to know they weren't alone in what they were carrying.

In those moments, my old version of "resolution-based" thinking would have made things worse.

It would have rushed in. Redirected. Minimized without meaning to.

But when I slowed down, when I stayed present instead of fixing, something different happened.

The conversation didn't stall. It deepened.

I learned that resolution often comes after understanding, not before it. And when understanding is given space, resolution tends to show up on its own, without being forced.

That was a hard lesson for me, because it required restraint, patience, and letting go of the idea that my value in the conversation was tied to having answers.

I also began to see how being prematurely resolution-based could feel dismissive to the other person, even when my tone was calm.

When someone is still in the middle of expressing something, offering a solution can sound like this:

I've heard enough. I already know what matters. Let's move on.

Even if that's not what you mean, that's often how it comes across.

And once someone feels dismissed, the conversation changes. They pull back. They become guarded. They stop sharing freely. Resolution becomes harder, not easier.

That's when I finally understood something critical:

Resolution is not an action you take. It's an outcome that emerges.

And it emerges only when the conversation has been honored first.

That insight forced me to redefine what it meant to be resolution-based.

It wasn't about speed. It wasn't about efficiency. It wasn't about ending things quickly.

It was about alignment.

Alignment with the other person. Alignment with the actual problem. Alignment with the moment.

When alignment is present, solutions make sense. When it isn't, even good solutions fail.

I'm learning that true resolution requires humility, the willingness to admit that I might not yet understand the problem well enough to solve it. It requires patience, the discipline to stay present even when the conversation feels inefficient. And it requires anchored thinking, the ability to slow myself down internally so I don't rush ahead of reality.

This chapter exists because I had to let go of the illusion that being resolution-based meant being right, fast, or decisive.

It means being aligned.

And alignment can't be rushed.

Application Layer, Chapter Two

Being resolution-based starts with asking the right question.

Before offering a solution, pause and ask yourself:
Do I fully understand what this person is experiencing?
Am I being asked to fix something, or to listen?
Am I trying to resolve the problem, or relieve my own discomfort?

One practical shift that has helped me is this: instead of offering a solution immediately, I ask, "What do you need from me right now?"

That question alone prevents countless misfires.

True resolution doesn't come from speed. It comes from presence.

Anchoring Scripture

"The purposes of a person's heart are deep waters,

but one who has insight draws them out."

Proverbs 20:5

Reflection Prompts, Chapter Two

When I say I'm "trying to help," what am I really trying to do?

How often do I jump to solutions before fully understanding the problem?

In what situations does my urgency increase, and why?

Where might slowing down actually lead to better outcomes?

What would change if I measured resolution by alignment instead of speed?

Opportunity, Chapter Two

When you release the pressure to fix, you create space for trust.

Trust invites honesty.
Honesty invites clarity.
Clarity makes resolution possible.

Being resolution-based isn't about ending conversations quickly.

It's about allowing the right ending to emerge.

Chapter Three

Listening Isn't Passive—It's Most Powerful

"He who answers before listening,

that is his folly and his shame."

Proverbs 18:13

Listening isn't about doing nothing. It's about doing the right thing first.

For a long time, I believed listening was something you did while waiting to speak.

I wouldn't have said it that way, of course. I would have told you I was a good listener. I paid attention. I nodded. I made eye contact. I stayed engaged. I didn't avoid conversations or check out when things got uncomfortable. I was present.

At least, that's how it felt.

But what I was actually doing most of the time wasn't listening, it was preparing.

Preparing to respond. Preparing to clarify. Preparing to explain. Preparing to defend.

I was listening with my guns already loaded.

And when you listen that way, something subtle but important happens, you stop hearing the whole thing.

I began to notice how often I reacted to fragments instead of meaning. A phrase would catch my attention and pull me out of the moment. A word would trigger an internal response. And before the other person finished their thought, my mind had already moved on.

I wasn't listening to understand. I was listening to respond.

That kind of listening feels active, but it's ineffective.

True listening requires restraint, the discipline to stay with someone's words all the way through, even when you feel the urge to jump in. And that restraint doesn't come naturally, especially when emotion is involved.

Listening isn't passive. It's powerful. All people have to be taught to listen and listening takes discipline. Listening takes practice. Listening takes control.

I saw this clearly in moments where conversations went sideways for no obvious reason.

Someone would be talking, and just a few words in, I'd feel tension rise in my body. My jaw would tighten. My shoulders would shift. I'd feel that familiar internal pressure, the need to correct, redirect, or clarify before something went wrong.

And often, something did go wrong.

Not because the conversation was dangerous, but because my thinking wasn't anchored enough to let it unfold.

When I interrupted, I wasn't just breaking the flow of the conversation. I was breaking trust.

The other person wasn't done yet. They hadn't finished their point. They hadn't finished connecting the dots.

And by stepping in too early, I communicated something without saying a word: my response matters more than your process.

That realization, although true, was uncomfortable.

Because I didn't interrupt out of arrogance. I interrupted out of anxiety.

I was afraid of being misunderstood. Afraid of being blamed. Afraid of the conversation drifting somewhere I couldn't control.

So, I tried to control it early.

But control is the enemy of listening.

I also began to notice how often silence felt risky to me. If I stayed quiet too long, I felt like I was conceding ground. If I didn't respond quickly, I worried I was being misread. Silence felt like agreement, or weakness, or loss of position.

But silence doesn't mean disengagement.

It means presence.

When I slowed myself down enough to actually listen, really listen, I noticed something else: people don't always know exactly what they're trying to say at first.

They need room to process out loud. They need time to connect their own thoughts. They need the safety of not being interrupted.

When that space exists, clarity emerges. When it doesn't, confusion deepens.

I started paying attention to how conversations changed when I stayed quiet just a little longer than I wanted to. When I let the other person finish completely. When I resisted the urge to jump in with my interpretation of what they meant.

Those conversations felt different.

They were calmer. They were clearer. They were less exhausting.

Not because I said less overall, but because I said less too soon.

I also noticed how often my interruptions redirected conversations in ways I didn't intend.

Someone would share something vulnerable, and my response, though well-meaning, would shift the focus back to me. To my explanation. To my logic. To my solution.

Suddenly, the conversation wasn't about understanding anymore. It was about managing reactions.

Listening isn't passive because it requires you to stay present without taking over.

It requires tolerating uncertainty. It requires resisting the urge to perform. It requires trusting that clarity will come if you don't rush it.

That's hard.

Especially if you're used to leading with your words.

But leadership doesn't start with speaking. It starts with listening and creating the space for them to be heard and understood.

I'm learning that some of the most influential moments in conversation aren't the things I say, they're the moments I don't interrupt. The pauses I allow. The silence I hold without filling.

That's where people feel seen. That's where they feel heard. That's where calm replaces tension.

Listening well doesn't make you invisible. It makes you trustworthy.

And trust changes everything.

The Cost of Half-Listening

What I didn't realize for a long time is that listening incorrectly doesn't just affect the moment, it creates work later.

There were conversations where I technically listened. I stayed quiet. I didn't interrupt. I nodded at the right times. On the surface, it looked like progress.

But afterward, something lingered.

The room felt unsettled. The connection felt incomplete. There was no explosion, just distance.

I would walk away thinking the conversation went fine, only to realize later that it hadn't actually resolved anything. Words were exchanged, but understanding wasn't. And because of that, the same issue would resurface, sometimes days later, sometimes weeks later, carrying more weight than it had the first time.

That's when I noticed the pattern: when listening isn't complete, conversations don't end, they pause.

Half-listening creates unfinished business.

The other person feels it too, even if they can't name it. They leave feeling partially heard, partially seen, and unsure whether it's worth reopening the conversation. So, they carry it instead.

And eventually, that weight shows up somewhere else, in tone, in distance, in frustration that seems to come out of nowhere.

Listening fully is an investment. Half-listening is a debt.

When Listening Breaks Down in Real Time

What surprised me most as I practiced listening longer wasn't how often I interrupted, it was how often I still communicated impatience without saying a word.

I could stay quiet and still derail a conversation.

My arms would cross. My posture would shift. My eyes would move away for just a second too long.

Listening isn't just about keeping your mouth closed. It's about regulating everything else that speaks first.

I remember a moment where I stayed silent through an entire explanation. I didn't interrupt. I didn't jump in. I did exactly what I thought I was supposed to do.

And yet, by the end of the conversation, the other person shut down.

Not because I talked too much, but because my body spoke for me.

Listening without internal discipline is just delayed reaction. It looks calm, but it isn't. It buys time, but it doesn't build safety.

True listening requires regulation.

Your face matches your intention. Your posture communicates openness. Your stillness feels supportive, not strained.

People don't just need to be heard. They need to feel safe while being heard.

And safety is created by being grounded.

Learning to Repair What Listening Missed

There were moments when I realized my listening failed only after the conversation was over.

Not during the exchange. Not in the moment. But later, when the silence felt heavier than it should have.

I would replay the conversation and notice what I missed. A pause I rushed past. A sentence I heard but didn't absorb. An emotion I acknowledged intellectually but never really sat with.

And by then, the damage was already done.

That's the part of listening no one talks about, the repair.

When listening breaks down, it doesn't always end in conflict. Sometimes it ends in quiet distance. A subtle shift. A hesitation that wasn't there before.

That's when the real work begins.

I had to learn how to go back, not to defend myself, not to explain my intentions, but to own what I missed.

“I don’t think I listened to you as fully as I thought I did.”
“I may have responded too quickly.”
“Can we come back to this?”

That required humility.

It meant letting someone say the same thing twice without irritation. It meant reopening conversations I assumed were finished.

Listening isn’t proven in the moment. It’s proven in what happens after.

Do people feel safe coming back to you? Do they trust you enough to try again?

That’s the measure.

Listening Reveals Who You Are

People don’t just learn how you communicate by what you say, they learn by how you listen.

Listening reveals patience or impatience. Security or defensiveness. Presence or performance.

Over time, people know who rushes them. They know who listens to respond. And they know who listens to understand.

Those distinctions matter.

People open up where they feel safe. Where they aren’t managed. Where their words aren’t immediately edited, corrected, or reframed.

Listening well builds quiet credibility. It doesn’t announce itself.

Being a good listener is the rock foundation on which good communication is built.

Listening doesn’t make you passive. It makes you grounded.

Application Layer, Chapter Three

Before your next meaningful conversation:
Let the other person finish completely
Count to three silently before responding
Ask one clarifying question before offering your perspective
Check your posture, breathing, and facial expression

Listening isn't about doing nothing. It's about doing the right thing first.

Anchoring Scripture

"He who answers before listening,

that is his folly and his shame."

Proverbs 18:13

Reflection Prompts, Chapter Three

Where do I feel the strongest urge to interrupt?

What emotions trigger my need to respond quickly?

How does my body communicate impatience even when I'm silent?

What would it look like to treat listening as leadership?

Who in my life might feel safer if I slowed down?

Opportunity, Chapter Three

Listening well builds trust.

Trust invites honesty.
Honesty invites clarity.
Clarity makes progress possible.
You don't need more to say.
You need more space to hear.
That's where strong communication begins.

Chapter Four

Emotional Discipline Creates Credibility

"A person's wisdom yields patience.

it is to one's glory to overlook an offense."

Proverbs 19:11

Discipline isn't about silence. It's about intentional direction

For a long time, I thought emotional discipline meant emotional control.

I assumed it was about not getting angry. Not raising your voice. Not reacting in ways you might regret later. If I stayed calm on the outside, I told myself I was doing well. If I didn't explode, shut down, or walk away, I counted that as progress.

But I've learned something different.

Emotional discipline isn't about suppressing emotion. It's about managing direction while emotion is present.

Because emotion doesn't wait for permission. It shows up in real time. In the middle of conversations. In moments where the stakes feel high. In situations where you don't get to pause the world and collect yourself neatly before responding.

That's where discipline actually matters.

Some of the conversations I regret did happen because I was angry. Others happened when I wasn't angry at all. I was still managing my emotions poorly.

Most of those moments didn't come from being out of control. They came from being emotionally unregulated while still talking. I was calm enough to speak, but not grounded enough to choose how I spoke.

That's a dangerous middle ground.

You feel justified. You sound reasonable. But you're not anchored.

And when that happens, emotion quietly takes the wheel.

When Emotion Accelerates the Conversation

I've noticed this pattern in myself more times than I care to admit. A conversation starts fine. I feel engaged. Present. Maybe even confident. Then something subtle shifts. A word hits wrong. A tone triggers something familiar. A feeling rises, pressure, defensiveness, urgency.

And suddenly, my internal speed increases.

I start talking faster. Explaining more. Clarifying sooner than needed. Trying to regain control of the moment.

On the outside, I still look composed. But internally, I've already crossed a line.

That's the moment emotional discipline is tested.

Not when things are calm. Not when everyone agrees. But when your body reacts before your mind catches up.

Emotional discipline isn't the absence of reaction, it's the ability to delay action long enough to choose direction.

Without that delay, conversations don't usually explode. They drift. They slide off track. They turn slightly sharp. Slightly defensive. Slightly misaligned.

And those "slight" shifts add up.

I used to think emotional discipline meant keeping things from escalating. Now I understand it means preventing misalignment before escalation ever happens.

A Moment I Failed, and What It Taught Me

There was a conversation where I didn't catch myself in time.

Nothing dramatic. No yelling. No slammed doors. Just a moment where I felt challenged, misunderstood, and quietly cornered. I responded quickly. Calmly. With words that sounded composed in my head.

But they weren't anchored.

I could see it in the other person's face before I fully heard it in their response. Their shoulders tightened. Their tone shifted. The conversation changed.

I had technically stayed "in control," but emotionally, I had already made the conversation unsafe.

And here's the hard part: at the time, I felt right.

That's the danger.

Undisciplined emotion doesn't always feel reckless. Sometimes it feels righteous. It convinces you that because you're calm, you're correct. Because you're articulate, you're aligned.

But alignment isn't determined by intent. It's determined by impact.

That conversation didn't fall apart because I was angry. It fell apart because my emotion led my words instead of informing them.

That's backwards thinking.

And backwards thinking always shows up as backwards talking.

When Emotion Becomes Instruction

Emotion itself isn't the problem. Unmanaged emotion is.

Emotion can be information, if you don't let it become instruction.

Fear can tell you something matters. Frustration can signal a boundary. Anxiety can point to uncertainty.

But none of those emotions should decide how you speak.

When emotion becomes instruction, words lose precision. Tone drifts. Body language tightens. Even accurate statements come out as accusations or defenses.

This is where many conversations go wrong quietly.

Backwards thinking tells you:
- I need to respond now
- I need to clarify before this goes any further
- If I don't speak up, I'll lose ground

Those thoughts feel urgent. They feel logical. They feel necessary.

They're usually wrong.

Urgency is often a symptom, not a solution.

Emotional Discipline as Leadership

This is where emotional discipline stops being personal and starts being leadership.

Whether you're leading in your home, your marriage, your workplace, or your community, people are always watching how you respond under pressure. Not just what you say, but how you regulate yourself while saying it.

Emotional discipline creates authority without demanding it.

People trust leaders who don't react impulsively. They feel safer bringing hard things to someone who can sit with tension without rushing to escape it.

I've learned that the strongest voices in a room are often the most restrained ones. Not silent, but intentional. Not passive, but observant.

A leader who reacts emotionally teaches everyone else to brace. A leader who stays disciplined teaches everyone else that he or she can be trusted.

That applies at home too.

Children learn regulation before they learn reasoning. Spouses feel safety before they feel resolution.

If emotional discipline is missing, even loving words can feel sharp. But when discipline leads, even hard truths feel manageable.

Discipline Is Not Suppression

I also had to confront how often I confused emotional discipline with emotional suppression.

I thought being disciplined meant ignoring what I felt or pushing it down. That never worked.

Suppressed emotion always leaks, in tone, in posture, in sarcasm, in impatience, in defensiveness you never intended to communicate.

- What belongs here?
- What needs to wait?
- What doesn't need to be said at all?

That organization is what allows conversations to stay productive even when emotions are present.

When Calm Is Actually a Mask

One of the hardest things I've had to learn is that calmness can be deceptive.

There were many conversations where I wasn't visibly angry. My voice was level. My words were composed. I didn't raise my tone or lose control. And because of that, I assumed I was being emotionally disciplined.

But calmness without anchoring is just restraint on the surface.

Internally, I was still racing.

I was tracking the conversation instead of experiencing it. Watching for threats. Preparing counterpoints. Holding my ground instead of holding a space for healing and understanding.

The conversation couldn't breathe.

What I didn't understand then is that emotional discipline isn't proven by how calm you appear. It's proven by how flexible you remain while calm.

If you're calm but unwilling to adjust... Calm but unwilling to listen... Calm but already decided...

That's not discipline. That's armor. And armor may protect you, but it builds a wall around you and keeps everyone else at a distance.

The Difference Between Restraint and Regulation

Restraint is holding back reaction. Regulation is guiding emotion.

I practiced restraint for years. I learned how to bite my tongue. How to pause long enough to avoid saying something reckless. How to keep conversations from escalating outwardly.

But restraint alone doesn't create safety.

In fact, restraint without regulation often makes people uneasy. They can feel the tension under the surface.

Regulation allows emotion to exist without letting it dominate. It means I can acknowledge internally what I'm feeling without needing the other person to absorb it.

I stopped asking, how do I keep this from going wrong? And started asking, how do I stay present while this unfolds? That shift alone changed how conversations felt on both sides.

When Discipline Feels Unfair

One of the quiet frustrations of emotional discipline is that it often feels one-sided.

There were moments when I was doing the work, slowing myself down, choosing restraint, regulating my tone, while the other person wasn't. They were emotional. Reactive. Frustrated.

And part of me wanted to say, why am I the only one trying here?

That's where emotional discipline gets tested. Because discipline isn't about fairness. It's about leadership.

Leadership doesn't wait for conditions to improve before showing up. It shows up first.

And emotional discipline is one of the clearest forms of leadership in conversation.

Being grounded doesn't guarantee the other person will follow immediately. But it does guarantee that you won't add fuel to the moment.

And more often than not, being grounded invites the other person to settle too, eventually.

Why Emotional Discipline Changes Outcomes

Here's the truth I had to face: Most of the conversations I regret didn't go wrong because of what was said. They went wrong because I wasn't settled when I said it.

When I'm disciplined emotionally:

• My tone stays open

- My posture stays relaxed
- My words stay precise

When I'm not:
- I overexplain
- I interrupt
- I defend prematurely

The difference isn't intelligence. It's discipline.

And discipline changes outcomes quietly, but consistently.

Application Layer, Chapter Four

When you feel emotion rise, don't speak yet.
Silently name what you're feeling:

• I feel defensive
• I feel anxious
• I feel frustrated

Naming emotion slows it down.

Then ask:
• What direction do I want this conversation to go?
• Will my next sentence move us there, or away from it?

Discipline isn't about silence.
It's about intentional direction.

Anchoring Scripture

"A person's wisdom yields patience,

it is to one's glory to overlook an offense."

Proverbs 19:11

Reflection Prompts, Chapter Four

What emotions most often push me to respond too quickly?
How does my body react before my words do?
Where do I mistake emotional honesty for emotional discipline?
What conversations in my life would benefit from slower responses?
Who might feel safer if I stayed more grounded more consistently?

Opportunity, Chapter Four

Emotional discipline creates credibility.

When people trust that you won't react impulsively, they speak more freely. When they speak more freely, understanding deepens. And when understanding deepens, conversations actually move forward.

Discipline doesn't remove emotion. It gives it direction, and purpose.

Chapter Five

Timing Is Everything

"There is a time for everything,

and a season for every activity under the heavens."

Ecclesiastes 3:1

Truth has seasons too.

For a long time, I believed that saying the right thing mattered more than when I said it.

If the words were true…
If the intention was good…
If the insight was helpful…

Then timing felt secondary. I told myself things like: It needed to be said. If I wait, I might lose the moment. If I don't address it now, it'll get worse. That logic felt responsible, almost mature. But it wasn't accurate.

Because I eventually learned something uncomfortable: you can say the right thing at the wrong time and that causes damage.

In fact, timing often determines whether truth feels like care or correction, whether honesty feels supportive or sharp, whether clarity feels grounding or threatening.

Most of the conversations I regret didn't go wrong because I said the wrong thing. They went wrong because I said the right thing too early, too fast, or too close to emotion.

When Urgency Masquerades as Wisdom

One of the clearest patterns I had to confront was how often urgency disguised itself as insight.

I would feel a realization hit mid-conversation, something important, something accurate, and my instinct was to release it immediately. I felt almost obligated to say it out loud, as if holding it back would be irresponsible.

But what I didn't realize then was this: insight doesn't automatically earn the right to be spoken. Timing determines whether insight arrives as wisdom or intrusion.

There were moments when someone was still processing, still emotional, still vulnerable, and I stepped in with clarity before they had finished feeling. Not because I didn't care, but because I thought clarity would help.

It rarely did.

Instead, I ruined a moment. The other person withdrew. The emotional window closed. And I was left wondering why something true hit so wrong.

The Difference Between Truth and Being Ready

This chapter exists because I had to separate truth from being ready to hear it.

Just because something is true doesn't mean it's receivable.

Just because something is helpful doesn't mean it's helpful now.

Just because something feels obvious to you doesn't mean the other person is in a position to hear it.

Being ready to hear something has nothing to do with how smart you are. It has everything to do with where you are emotionally.

When someone is overwhelmed, timing matters more than precision.

When someone is defensive, timing matters more than logic.

When someone is hurting, timing matters more than correctness.

I had to learn that forcing truth into an unreceptive moment doesn't make it the truth, it makes it a distraction.

Why "Now" Is Often the Wrong Answer

One of the most honest questions I had to start asking myself was this: Why does this need to be said right now?

Sometimes the answer was legitimate.

But often, it wasn't.

More often, the real answer was:

I'm uncomfortable with silence

I want relief from tension

I feel misunderstood

I want resolution now

Those reasons feel urgent, but they aren't always respectful.

Urgency is often about me.

Timing is about us.

And respect lives in the difference.

Timing Is Emotional Awareness in Action

I used to think respect showed up in tone. Then I learned it shows up in timing and in tone.

Respect asks:

Is this person regulated enough to receive this?

Has this moment earned this level of honesty?

Am I speaking to help, or to discharge my own pressure?

I learned this most clearly in moments where I waited.

Not forever, just long enough.

And when I eventually spoke, the same words hit differently. Not because they changed, but because the moment did.

That taught me something critical: waiting doesn't weaken truth. It strengthens it.

When Timing Is Ignored, Power Shifts

Another thing I didn't expect was how badly mistimed words can shift power in a conversation. When you speak too soon, you take the moment away from the other person. That can feel controlling, even if it's unintentional. And once someone feels controlled, they stop offering honesty. They start protecting themselves. Timing preserves dignity. Poor timing erodes it.

Learning to Hold Without Withholding

This chapter isn't about avoiding hard conversations. It's about holding insight without weaponizing it.

There's a difference between withholding and waiting.

Withholding is fear-based.

Waiting is discipline-based.

Waiting says, this matters enough to say it well.

Withholding says, this is too risky to say at all.

Learning that difference changed how I showed up. I stopped rushing conversations toward closure. I stopped inserting clarity mid-emotion. I stopped treating silence as failure.

And something surprising happened: people opened up more.

Not because I spoke less truth, but because I honored timing.

Timing Builds Trust

Trust doesn't grow from accuracy alone. It grows from being in harmony with the emotional state of the other person.

When people sense that you can feel the moment, read it, respect it, wait with it, they trust you with more: more honesty, more vulnerability, more complexity.

They don't brace for your insight. They invite it.

That's the difference timing makes.

A Moment Where Waiting Changed Everything

One moment clarified this lesson for me in a way theory never could.

I remember a conversation where everything in me wanted to speak. I had clarity, real clarity. I knew what the issue was, why it mattered, and what needed to change. The words were already formed. They felt responsible. Necessary. Loving, even.

But the person across from me wasn't finished yet.

They were still sorting through emotion. Still finding language. Still vulnerable in a way that doesn't invite interruption without consequence.

I felt the familiar pressure rise, the urge to help by explaining, to stabilize the moment by naming truth, to move things forward so it wouldn't spiral.

And for once, I didn't.

I stayed quiet longer than I felt comfortable. Not passive. Not withdrawn. Present, but in control.

What happened next surprised me.

They kept talking.

And as they did, the clarity I was so eager to share became less urgent, not because it was wrong, but because it was incomplete. There were layers I hadn't heard yet. Nuances I would have missed. Context that mattered.

Had I spoken when I wanted to, I would have redirected the conversation toward my understanding instead of allowing theirs to finish forming.

By the time the communication was complete the same truth hit differently. Softer. Cleaner. More connected. It didn't interrupt anything, it aligned with it.

And it was received.

That moment taught me something I still return to:

Sometimes the most disciplined thing you can do with truth is wait until it belongs to the moment, not just to you.

Waiting didn't dilute what I had to say. It refined it.

And more importantly, it preserved trust.

When You Get It Wrong (And You Will)

Even now, I still misjudge timing sometimes.

I still speak too soon.

I still underestimate emotion.

I still rush moments that need space.

But I've learned to repair timing mistakes differently.

Instead of defending the truth of what I said, I acknowledge the timing of it.

Making the person matter more to you than making your point is what honoring timing really communicates.

Those statements restore safety faster than explanation ever could.

Because they say: You matter more than my point.

And that's what timing really communicates.

Application Layer, Chapter Five

Before speaking something difficult, ask:
Does this need to be said now, or does it need to be said well?
Am I responding to the moment, or my discomfort?
Has this person finished processing?

Practice this discipline:
If emotion is high, slow down.
If defensiveness is present, wait.
If clarity feels urgent, pause.

Timing isn't delay. It's respect in motion.

Anchoring Scripture

"There is a time for everything,

and a season for every activity under the heavens."

Ecclesiastes 3:1

Reflection Prompts, Chapter Five

Where do I feel pressure to speak before the moment is ready?

How do I react to silence in emotional conversations?

What truths have I said too early in the past?

How might waiting increase impact rather than reduce it?

Who in my life needs timing more than explanation?

Opportunity, Chapter Five

When you honor timing:
People feel respected
Conversations feel safer
Truth goes deeper

Timing doesn't dilute honesty.
It dignifies it.

And when truth is delivered with respect, it doesn't need to fight to be heard.

Chapter Six

Why Timing Matters More Than Truth

There is a time to be silent and a time to speak."

Ecclesiastes 3:7

Wisdom isn't knowing what to say.

It's knowing when.

The last chapter was about whether the moment was ready. This one's about something harder, being right, and choosing the relationship over the point anyway.

There are moments when you can say the right thing and you still can be wrong. Not because the words are inaccurate. Not because the point lacks merit. Not because the truth isn't real. But because the moment can't receive it.

For a long time, I believed truth carried its own authority, that if something needed to be said, it should be said as soon as it became clear. I told myself that delaying truth was avoidance, that waiting was weakness, that holding back meant compromising honesty.

I was wrong.

What I've learned, sometimes painfully, is that truth without timing doesn't build clarity. It creates resistance.

And resistance changes everything.

When Truth Becomes a Weapon

Some of the most damaging conversations I've had didn't come from lies or manipulation. They came from truth delivered too early, too sharply, or too insistently.

I would speak honestly, sometimes even gently, and still watch the other person shut down. Their posture changed. Their tone hardened. And I would leave confused, replaying the moment, asking myself the same question:

How could telling the truth make things worse? The answer wasn't in what I said. It was in when I said it.

Truth doesn't travel alone. It arrives in a nervous system, in emotion, in context. And if the person hearing it isn't safe, or isn't ready, truth doesn't feel like clarity, it feels like an attack.

Even when it's accurate. Even when it's necessary. Even when it's inevitable.

Timing determines whether truth feels like guidance or judgment.

The Illusion of "They Need to Hear This"

One of the most convincing lies I told myself was this:

They need to hear this right now.

That sentence sounds responsible, mature, even. But underneath it was often something else entirely: urgency rooted in my own discomfort.

I needed relief. I needed the tension gone. I needed resolution.

And instead of recognizing that, I wrapped my urgency in the language of honesty.

That's a dangerous move.

Because when you convince yourself that urgency equals necessity, you stop checking timing. You stop reading the room. You stop asking whether the moment can actually hold what you're about to say.

You tell the truth, but you tell it alone.

Why Being Ready Comes Before Accuracy

Something can be one hundred percent true and still be received as wrong. Not because the content is flawed, but because the other person isn't there yet.

Being ready means you're regulated, not flooded. You're open instead of defensive, curious instead of afraid. You feel safe enough to actually hear what's being said.

It looks like safety instead of a threat.

Without those conditions, truth doesn't clarify, it escalates.

I've learned that before truth can do its work, the environment has to be right. And that environment isn't external, it's internal, for both people.

You don't introduce depth into chaos. You don't introduce correction into fear. You don't introduce clarity into defensiveness. You stabilize first. Then you speak.

The Cost of Being "Right" Too Soon

Being right too early often costs more than being wrong. It costs trust. It costs openness. It costs future conversations.

I've seen this pattern repeat itself: a moment where I could have waited but didn't. A moment where I could have prioritized safety but chose accuracy instead. And the result wasn't clarity, it was distance.

Once distance enters a conversation, truth has to work twice as hard. Not because the truth changed, but because the relationship did.

People remember how something made them feel long after they forget the exact words that were said. Timing shapes that memory.

When Silence Is Strategic, Not Avoidant

This distinction took me years to understand.

Silence isn't always avoidance. Sometimes it's discipline.

There were moments when I knew exactly what I wanted to say, and I didn't say it. Not because I was afraid, but because I could see the moment was unstable. Any truth I introduced would become ammunition instead of insight.

Waiting didn't weaken the truth. It protected it.

When the moment came later, calmer, more grounded, safer, the same words hit completely differently.

That taught me something essential:

Truth doesn't expire because it waits.

But trust often does if it doesn't wait.

Truth Needs a Pathway

Truth doesn't just need accuracy. It needs access.

Access is created through:
emotional safety
relational trust
demonstrated listening
patience

Without a pathway, truth hits a wall. I've learned to ask myself a different question now. Not Is this true? But, Is there a path for this truth to be received right now?

If the answer is no, waiting is wisdom, not compromise.

Holding Truth vs. Withholding It

This is where timing often gets misunderstood.

Holding truth is not the same as withholding it.

Withholding it is avoidance. Holding it is stewardship of the moment.

Holding truth means you take responsibility not just for accuracy, but for impact. You stay attentive to the moment, the relationship, and the capacity of the person in front of you.

Withholding avoids discomfort. Holding prepares for clarity.

That distinction changed how I see restraint. It isn't cowardice. It's care.

Why Timing Is an Act of Love

When you care about someone, timing becomes part of respect.

You don't force insight. You don't rush awareness. You don't demand understanding on your schedule.

You honor process.

That doesn't mean avoiding hard conversations forever. It means choosing moments that give those conversations a chance to succeed.

Timing says:

I care about how this is received, not just that it's said.

I value connection as much as clarity.

I'm willing to wait for alignment.

That kind of restraint builds trust far faster than blunt honesty ever will.

Truth as Self-Regulation (The Trap)

There's a subtle trap I've fallen into more times than I want to admit using truth to anchor myself instead of serving the moment.

The words are accurate. The insight is valid. The observation is real. But the timing is wrong.

In those moments, truth becomes less about clarity and more about control. I'm not offering it because it's needed, I'm offering it because I need relief. Relief from tension. Relief from uncertainty. Relief from sitting inside a conversation that hasn't settled yet.

Truth used that way stops being a bridge and starts being about me. It stops serving the moment and starts serving my need for relief. That's the distinction I had to learn.

When Timing Changes the Outcome

I've seen the difference timing makes.

I've watched conversations that would have collapsed hold together because I waited. I've seen defensiveness soften because I didn't rush. I've felt trust increase simply because I respected the moment.

Timing doesn't dilute truth. It delivers it. Truth doesn't lose value by waiting.

But it does lose impact when it's rushed. Holding truth doesn't make you weaker.

It proves you're strong enough to wait.

When truth serves the moment, not self, it doesn't need force. It arrives naturally. It's received instead of resisted.

And it does what truth is meant to do in the first place:

It brings alignment, not relief. Not distance. But closeness and trust.

Application Layer, Chapter Six

Before speaking a difficult truth, pause and ask:
Is the other person emotionally ready to receive truth?
Do they feel heard already?
Is there trust in the room right now?
Am I speaking for clarity, or relief?

If the moment feels unstable, wait.

Timing isn't avoidance.
It's preparation.

Anchoring Scripture

"There is a time to be silent and a time to speak."

Ecclesiastes 3:7

Reflection Prompts, Chapter Six

When do I feel the strongest urge to speak immediately?
How often do I confuse urgency with responsibility?
What truths in my life might need better timing, not more force?
How does waiting change the way my words are received?
Where could patience increase impact?

Opportunity, Chapter Six

When you honor timing, truth becomes collaborative instead of confrontational.
People don't brace.
They listen.
They stay.

And when truth arrives in the right moment, it doesn't have to fight to be heard.
It's welcomed.

Chapter Seven

When Words Are Used as Weapons (Even Quietly)

"The tongue has the power of life and death,

and those who love it will eat its fruit."

Proverbs 18:21

Words always produce something.

Choose carefully what you grow

For a long time, I believed that as long as I wasn't yelling, I was communicating well.

I wasn't aggressive. I wasn't explosive. I wasn't losing control. I chose my words carefully. I kept my tone even. On the surface, everything looked disciplined.

But something still felt off. Conversations would end without resolution, not in obvious ways, but in subtle ones. The other person would go quiet. Not shut down completely, just different. Less open. More guarded. I told myself it was because the conversation was difficult. Because truth can be uncomfortable. Because not everyone likes clarity. But over time, that explanation stopped working. Because if clarity was the goal, why did people leave conversations feeling smaller instead of heard?

That question forced me to look at something I didn't want to see. I wasn't always using words to connect. Sometimes, I was using them to control.

Not loudly. Not cruelly. Quietly.

I had learned how to sound reasonable while steering conversations in my favor. How to phrase questions that boxed people in. How to present conclusions as inevitabilities. How to pause in ways that applied pressure instead of space.

I wasn't trying to hurt anyone. But I was trying to manage outcomes. And management masquerading as communication is still manipulation.

That realization was uncomfortable because I prided myself on being thoughtful. I believed intentional language equaled healthy communication. But intention alone doesn't determine impact.

Words can be weaponized without being raised. They can dominate without shouting. They can wound while sounding calm. That's what made it hard to see. Weaponized words don't feel aggressive to the person using them. They feel efficient.

I began noticing how often my language subtly positioned me above the conversation instead of inside it. How often my phrasing left the other person with fewer options instead of more clarity. How often my "logic" arrived before their experience did.

That's when I understood something critical: control doesn't always look forceful. Sometimes it looks polished.

There was also a quieter cost I didn't notice at first, the cost to myself.

When you communicate with subtle control, you're never fully at rest. You're monitoring reactions. Tracking responses. Managing tone, pacing outcomes. You're not present, you're performing presence instead of practicing it.

That's exhausting.

I would leave conversations mentally spent, even when nothing "bad" happened. No argument. No blowup. Just a lingering tightness. A sense that I had been on the whole time.

For me that was a key indicator.

Healthy conversations don't drain you because you're not guarding anything. You're not calculating leverage. You're not bracing for pushback. You're simply present.

Weaponized communication requires vigilance.

Disciplined communication requires trust.

And trust brings rest. And rest in relationships brings longevity.

When Backwards Thinking Arms the Words

What made this so hard for me to see was that none of this started at my mouth. It started in my head.

Backwards thinking had already taken position long before I spoke. I had already framed the situation. Already decided what mattered. Already determined what the "real issue" was, often without realizing I had done it.

So, when I finally spoke, my words were calm.

But they were armed.

I wasn't yelling.

I wasn't emotional.

I wasn't out of control.

But I was aiming as if I was pointing a gun and its name was protection.

That's the danger of backwards thinking, it convinces you that because you're calm, you're safe. Because you're articulate, you're right. Because you're quiet, you're more disciplined.

In reality, that thinking had already moved ahead of the relationship.

Instead of entering the conversation to understand, I entered it to be heard. Instead of listening to learn, I listened to correct. Instead of staying curious, I stayed prepared. I stayed armed.

That's how words become weapons quietly.

Not because they're harsh, but because they're deployed.

Backwards thinking loads the gun. Backwards talking pulls the trigger.

And the damage isn't immediate.

It's cumulative. It becomes a bad seed that begins to grow bad communication.

Each conversation where control replaces curiosity teaches the other person something without saying it out loud. And continued bad communication is the beginning of the end of the relationship.

Precision Without Care

Another thing I had to confront was how often I mistook precision for care.

I was articulate. Thoughtful. Intentional with my words. But precision without compassion still cuts, cleanly, quietly, and often more deeply.

People don't just hear what you say. They feel how safe they are while hearing it.

I had moments where I said exactly the right thing, but in a way that made the other person feel exposed instead of supported. Corrected instead of understood. Managed instead of met.

That's when I realized something important: language can be technically accurate and still emotionally careless.

Care shows up in pacing. In pauses. In allowing the other person to stay whole while the truth is being spoken.

Weaponized words remove dignity.

Disciplined words preserve it.

Silence Can Be a Weapon Too

I also began to notice how silence functions differently depending on intention.

There's silence that creates space for openness and bonding.

And there's silence that applies pressure.

I had used both.

Sometimes I would go quiet not to reflect, but to signal disappointment. To let the weight of my unspoken judgment hang in the room. I didn't raise my voice. I didn't say anything unkind. I just withheld.

That silence wasn't helpful.

It was strategic.

And strategic silence is still control.

That realization forced me to reexamine not just my words, but my absence of words. Why I paused. Why I waited. Why I stayed quiet.

Was I creating room, or applying pressure? Discipline demands honesty at that level.

Because communication isn't just verbal.

It's atmospheric.

People feel what you say sometimes more than they hear what you say. They can sense your intention. And they adjust accordingly.

And when people adjust to protect themselves, intimacy fades and a breakdown in the relationship has begun.

Slowing the Internal Tempo

What changed things for me was learning to slow my internal tempo before speaking, not to sound better, but to prepare myself to listen. To let my nervous system settle before my mouth opened.

That pause, sometimes just a few seconds, changed everything.

It interrupted old patterns.

It broke urgency.
It created choice.
In that pause, I could ask myself:
Am I trying to connect, or correct?
Am I speaking from clarity or from control?
Will this build trust, or just prove a point?

That pause became a line of defense against weaponized language. Because most harmful words aren't planned. They're reflexive. And reflex disappears when awareness is present.

Repair Builds Trust Faster Than Precision

I also learned that accountability in communication doesn't mean never missing, it means repairing quickly when you do.

There were times I caught myself mid-sentence. Times I stopped and said, "That came out sharper than I intended." Times I owned the tone of my voice instead of defending what came out of my mouth.

Those moments didn't weaken my position. They strengthened trust.

Repair builds credibility faster than perfection ever could.

What surprised me most was how often people responded with relief instead of resistance when I owned my missteps, as if they had been bracing for justification and were grateful not to receive it.

Most people aren't looking to win conversations. They're looking to feel safe inside them.

Weaponized words make people brace.
Disciplined words let them breathe.
And breathing changes everything.

Where Weaponized Words Show Up Most

For me, this showed up most clearly at home.

With my wife, it often sounded like leadership but felt like correction. I thought I was being clear. I thought I was being helpful. But clarity without care feels like judgment, even when you don't mean it that way.

I would explain too quickly. Clarify too early. Try to resolve before she had finished saying what she needed to say.

And when she responded, not to what I meant, but to what she heard me say. I would feel misunderstood. That's when I'd start explaining again. Backpedaling and explaining even more.

That's not connection. That's control trying to clean up after itself.

With my children, it sometimes looked like a dictatorship demanding good behavior, without first finding out why they chose the behavior in the first place. And the result wasn't respect. It was distance.

At work, it showed up as decisiveness without asking for any input. Conversations ended efficiently, but not collaboratively.

People complied. They didn't engage.

Weaponized words don't always cause conflict.

They cause compliance without connection.

And compliance never builds trust.

What finally changed things for me wasn't learning new language, it was learning when not to deploy it. Letting conversations breathe. Letting people finish. Letting discomfort exist without trying to manage it away.

Because when words are no longer used to steer, people stop bracing. When control steps back, trust steps forward.

Application Layer, Chapter Seven

Before speaking in a tense or important conversation, pause and ask:

Am I trying to move this conversation forward, or shut it down?

Am I asking a question to understand, or to corner?

Am I speaking from a settled place, or from urgency?

Practice replacing statements with invitations:

Instead of "This is what's really happening," try "Help me understand how you're seeing this."

Instead of "Don't you think…," try "Can you walk me through your thinking?"

Pay attention to your tone and remember your purpose.

Communication discipline isn't about saying less.

It's about saying what belongs.

Anchoring Scripture

"The tongue has the power of life and death,

and those who love it will eat its fruit."

Proverbs 18:21

Reflection Prompts, Chapter Seven

Where do I use questions to steer instead of understanding?
When do I confuse clarity with control?
How does my silence communicate intention?
What conversations feel draining, and why?
What would change if I valued trust over precision?
Are you able to bring rest to your partner?
Do you notice when your communication starts to deplete intimacy.

Opportunity, Chapter Seven

Disciplined words create safety.

Safety invites honesty.
Honesty deepens connection.
Connection sustains relationships.

You don't need sharper words.
You need calmer ones.

That's where real strength lives.

Chapter Eight

When Clarity Feels Like Conflict

"Speak the truth in love."

Ephesians 4:15

Truth without love wounds.

Love without truth weakens.

Clarity requires both.

I used to believe clarity guaranteed peace.

If I could just explain myself clearly enough, choose the right words, frame the thought correctly, say it calmly, then the conversation would go the way I intended. Misunderstandings would dissolve. Tension would ease. We would move forward aligned.

That belief made sense to me.

Clarity felt responsible. Mature. Necessary. I told myself that confusion caused conflict, so clarity must resolve it. If people understood me, things would be fine. If they didn't, then the problem was incomplete communication.

But experience taught me something different.

Clarity doesn't always feel peaceful.
Sometimes, clarity feels like conflict.

Not because it's wrong, but because it disrupts something that was being quietly tolerated.

I began noticing how often tension surfaced after I was clear, not before it. Conversations didn't always go sideways because of misunderstanding. Sometimes they went sideways because clarity exposed a truth neither person was ready to deal with.

And I wasn't prepared for that.

The Myth That Clarity Is Gentle

I used to believe that if I spoke gently, clarity would arrive gently.

But clarity isn't inherently soft. It's precise. And precision has edges.

When you name something accurately, you remove the gray area. And uncertainty, while uncomfortable, often acts as a buffer. It gives people room to avoid what they're not ready to face. It allows unresolved things to coexist without being addressed directly.

Clarity removes that buffer.

When you say what you mean clearly, you don't just communicate information, you introduce responsibility. You force the conversation to move somewhere. And movement creates friction.

That friction isn't failure. It's exposure.

I had to learn that clarity often feels like conflict before it creates alignment.

Why Clarity Triggers Resistance

I started paying attention to what happened internally when clarity showed up in conversations, mine or someone else's.

Resistance didn't always come from disagreement. Often, it came from disruption.

Clarity disrupts:

- familiar patterns
- unspoken agreements
- emotional shortcuts
- assumptions we've been living inside without naming

When clarity enters the room, people can no longer rely on implication. They have to respond to what's actually being said.

That's uncomfortable.

So instead of hearing clarity as information, people often hear it as confrontation.

And sometimes… they're not wrong.

Because clarity does confront things:

- avoidance
- denial
- emotional inertia
- half-truths that were easier to live with

That doesn't make clarity aggressive. But it does make it activate.

The Difference Between Aggression and Accuracy

One of the most important distinctions I've had to learn is this:

Accuracy is not aggression.

But when someone isn't ready for accuracy, it will feel aggressive anyway.

I used to back away from clarity when I felt that reaction. I'd soften my words. Walk them back. Add disclaimers. Try to reduce the discomfort in the room.

Sometimes that was wisdom. Other times, it was fear.

Fear of being seen as difficult. Fear of being misunderstood. Fear of creating conflict where I wanted peace.

But avoiding clarity doesn't prevent conflict. It delays it.

And delayed conflict almost always costs more.

When Clarity Forces a Decision

Another thing clarity does, it forces decisions that uncertainty allows people to postpone.

When something is vague, you can keep pretending it will resolve itself. When it's clear, you have to choose how you'll respond.

That's why clarity often escalates emotion.

Not because the message is harsh, but because it removes hiding places.

I had to confront the fact that some of the tension I experienced after being clear wasn't caused by my tone or my timing. It was caused by the fact that clarity required something of the other person, and of me.

And not everyone welcomes that moment.

Learning to Stay Grounded When Clarity Gets Loud

This chapter exists because I used to mistake emotional reaction as a signal that clarity was wrong.

If the conversation became tense, I assumed I had failed. If someone became defensive, I assumed I had pushed too hard. If things felt uncomfortable, I assumed I should retreat.

But clarity doesn't always produce immediate calm. Sometimes it produces noise first.

The discipline isn't avoiding that noise. The discipline is staying grounded inside it.

That's where anchored thinking matters most.

Because when clarity feels like conflict, your instinct will be to:

- explain more
- justify yourself
- soften the truth
- retreat from what you said

And sometimes that instinct undoes the very clarity you worked to establish.

Clarity Without Anchoring Becomes Weaponized

I also had to acknowledge the other side of this.

Clarity without anchoring can become sharp.

If clarity is driven by frustration, it arrives as accusation. If it's driven by urgency, it comes out as pressure. If it's driven by ego, it's received as dominance.

That's not clarity, that's emotional leakage wearing the costume of truth.

So, the question isn't whether to be clear. The question is who is leading your clarity.

Anchored thinking allows clarity to remain clean. Unanchored emotion turns clarity into a blade.

What Anchored Clarity Sounds Like

Anchored clarity doesn't rush. It doesn't posture. It doesn't perform.

It sounds like:

- "I want to be clear about what I need."
- "This is how I'm experiencing this."
- "I don't want to leave this implied."

It doesn't overexplain.
It doesn't apologize for existing.
It doesn't demand agreement.

Anchored clarity respects the other person, while still honoring yourself.

And that balance is hard.

Why Some Conversations Can't Stay Comfortable

One of the most freeing realizations I've had is this:

Some conversations are not meant to stay comfortable.

Comfort isn't the goal.
Understanding is.

And sometimes, understanding requires discomfort on the way through.

When clarity enters a space that has been held together by silence, the silence will protest. When clarity names something that's been avoided, avoidance will push back.

That doesn't mean you did it wrong. It means you touched something real.

Learning Not to Chase Resolution Immediately

This was especially hard for me.

When clarity created tension, I wanted to resolve it immediately. I wanted to smooth things over, restore calm, reassure everyone, including myself, that things were okay.

But immediate resolution often undermines clarity.

Sometimes clarity needs time to settle. Sometimes the other person needs space to process. Sometimes you need space to stay anchored instead of retreating.

Resolution doesn't always come in the same conversation clarity enters.

That took discipline to accept.

Clarity as an Act of Respect

I'm learning to see clarity differently now.

Not as confrontation.
Not as conflict.

But as respect.

Respect for myself, by not hiding.

Respect for the other person, by not manipulating with vagueness.

Respect for the relationship, by not letting important things remain unspoken.

Clarity says:

"I trust you enough to be honest."

"I trust myself enough to stand by what I mean."

"I trust the relationship enough to let it mature."

That kind of clarity may feel uncomfortable at first. But it builds something stronger underneath.

There was a moment I remember clearly, not because it was dramatic, but because it was subtle.

I had finally slowed myself down. My thinking was anchored. My words were composed. I wasn't defensive. I wasn't rushed. I wasn't trying to win anything. I was simply clear.

And the response I got wasn't relief. It was resistance.

The other person stiffened. Their tone changed. Not sharply, but noticeably. What I said wasn't wrong. It wasn't unkind. It wasn't careless. But it disrupted something they were holding onto, and clarity has a way of doing that.

That moment taught me something important: clarity doesn't always feel good to the person receiving it, especially if they're not ready for it.

I used to believe that if I communicated clearly enough, things would automatically smooth out. That clarity would always be welcomed. That understanding would immediately follow.

That's not how it works.

Clarity doesn't force agreement.
It reveals reality.

And sometimes, what clarity reveals creates discomfort before it creates alignment.

In the past, when I sensed that resistance, I would backtrack. Soften unnecessarily. Over-explain. Try to make the clarity more digestible so it wouldn't cost the connection.

Now I understand something different.

Clarity is not aggression. Discomfort is not danger. Resistance is not failure.

That moment wasn't a breakdown. It was a boundary forming in real time.

And learning to stay grounded there, without apologizing for clarity or escalating to defend it, was one of the hardest and most important shifts I've made.

Application Layer, Chapter Eight

Before choosing clarity in a conversation, pause and ask:

The Anchored Clarity Practice

When clarity feels risky, most people either soften too much or sharpen too fast. Neither builds trust.

Here's a simple discipline I'm learning to use instead:

1. Anchor Before You Speak
Ask yourself one question silently:
Am I grounded, or am I trying to control the outcome?
If you feel rushed internally, clarity will come out sideways.

2. Deliver Without Padding
Say the thing plainly, without over-explaining, justifying, or cushioning it to manage the reaction.
Clarity loses power when it's wrapped in apology.

3. Stay Present After You Speak
This is the hardest part.
Don't rush to fix discomfort.
Don't retreat.
Don't escalate.
Let clarity sit long enough to be processed.

Anchored clarity isn't about getting agreement.
It's about staying aligned with yourself while giving the other person space to respond honestly.

- Am I clear because I'm anchored, or because I'm frustrated?

- Am I naming something that needs to be named, or reacting to pressure?
- Can I stay grounded if this creates discomfort?

Practice delivering clarity without chasing immediate relief.

Say what belongs.
Then stop.

Let the clarity do its work.

Anchoring Scripture

"Speak the truth in love."

Ephesians 4:15

Reflection Prompts, Chapter Eight

1. Where do I avoid clarity to keep peace?
2. When clarity creates tension, how do I usually respond?
3. What truths have I softened out of fear?
4. How does my body react when conversations become uncomfortable?
5. What would it look like to trust clarity instead of retreating from it?

Opportunity, Chapter Eight

Clarity is not the enemy of connection.

Avoidance is.

When clarity is anchored, it doesn't destroy relationships, it reveals whether they're strong enough to grow.

And growth always begins with something being named.

Chapter Nine

When Clarity Feels Risky

"Speaking the truth in love, we are to grow up in every way."

Ephesians 4:15

Truth and love are not opposites.
They are partners.

The last chapter was about how it's received once I've finally said it. This one's about what stops me before I ever get the words out.

For a long time, I believed that if something needed to be said, saying it was the hardest part.

I thought the challenge was courage, the willingness to speak up, address the issue, or step into an uncomfortable conversation. And in some ways, that was true. Silence can feel heavy. Avoidance can feel dishonest. Carrying unspoken thoughts has a cost.

But what I've learned is this: clarity isn't avoided because people don't know what to say. It's avoided because clarity feels risky.

Not risky in a dramatic way. Not dangerous in an obvious sense. Risky in the quieter, more personal ways that matter most.

Clarity risks changing how you’re seen. Clarity risks disappointing someone. Clarity risks being misunderstood, judged, or rejected. Clarity risks exposing where you actually stand.

And for people who care deeply about relationships, harmony, and connection, that risk can feel heavier than silence.

I’ve felt that tension more times than I can count.

There were moments where I knew exactly what needed to be said. Not vaguely. Not eventually. Exactly. The words were clear in my head. The boundary was clear. The truth was clear.

But my body resisted.

My chest tightened. My timing slipped. My delivery softened too much, or became overly careful. And instead of clarity, I offered fragments. Hints. Half-statements that left room for interpretation and not room for my truth.

I told myself I was being thoughtful. I told myself I was being patient. I told myself I was choosing the right moment.

But often, what I was really doing was delaying clarity because I didn’t want to deal with the impact.

Clarity feels risky because it removes uncertainty, and while uncomfortable, it gives us cover.

When things are unclear, you can still be liked. When things are unclear, you can still belong. When things are unclear, you can still adjust your position later.

Clarity closes those escape routes.

And that's why it requires more discipline than silence ever does.

The Difference Between Knowing and Saying

When You Stay Clear Internally with Your Thoughts but Vague Externally.

One of the quietest forms of self-betrayal is knowing exactly what you believe and refusing to let it take shape out loud.

I didn't always notice it in real time. It showed up afterward, when I replayed conversations and realized I had been clear with myself but cautious with everyone else.

I would leave interactions thinking, they should have understood what I meant, while knowing I never actually said it.

That gap matters.

Internal clarity without external expression creates invisible tension. You feel aligned in your own mind but disconnected in your relationships. And because no one else has access to your internal reasoning, they respond to what you allow, not what you believe.

That's where resentment quietly grows.

Not because others are ignoring your needs, but because they were never clearly stated.

I had to face an uncomfortable truth: people can't honor boundaries they don't know exist. They can't respect positions you only imply. And they can't align with expectations you never state.

Clarity isn't just about honesty, it's about responsibility.

When you stay vague externally, you force others to guess. And when people guess wrong, you end up carrying frustration they never agreed to hold.

That's not kindness.
That's confusion.

One of the most uncomfortable realizations I've had is how often I confused internal clarity with external honesty.

I knew where I stood, but I didn't always let others know where I stood.

Not because I was deceptive. Not because I wanted to manipulate outcomes. But because I wanted to minimize disruption.

I wanted conversations to go smoothly. I wanted relationships to stay stable. I wanted to avoid emotional fallout.

So instead of stating things plainly, I layered them.

I softened statements that needed firmness. I delayed conversations that needed immediacy. I framed truths as questions to reduce their weight.

And while that approach felt safer in the moment, it created something else over time: misalignment.

People responded to what I said, not to what I meant. Expectations formed around what I allowed, not what I intended. Tension accumulated because clarity was postponed.

And eventually, clarity arrived anyway, just later, heavier, and more complicated.

That's the cost of clarity delayed: it doesn't disappear. It compounds.

Why Clarity Triggers Fear

Clarity forces commitment.

Once you say something clearly, you can't pretend you didn't mean it. Once a boundary is named, it exists. Once a truth is spoken, it reshapes the relationship.

That permanence is intimidating.

Especially if you've learned, consciously or unconsciously, that being clear can lead to conflict, rejection, or loss.

Most communication skills or lack of are shaped when you are a young child.

Many of us learned early that clarity came with consequences.

Say what you really think, and you might be corrected. Say what you really feel, and you might be dismissed. Say what you really need, and you might be told it's too much.

So, we adapt.

We become articulate without being direct. Thoughtful without being firm. Engaged without being honest.

We learn how to talk around things instead of through them.

And over time, that pattern starts to feel normal, even responsible.

But clarity isn't irresponsibility.
It's alignment.

And alignment always carries risk because it removes the buffer of uncertainty.

Clarity also introduces something many people quietly fear finality.

Once something is said clearly, it creates a before and an after. Uncertainty keeps doors open. Clarity closes some of them.

But not every open door is healthy.

Some doors keep you circling instead of moving forward. Some doors quietly drain energy because they require constant emotional negotiation.

Clarity doesn't close doors to punish anyone.
It closes doors that no longer serve you.

And that kind of closure isn't cruel.
It's stabilizing.

When Timing Becomes an Excuse

One of the most convincing ways we avoid clarity is by waiting for the "right time."

I've told myself that story many times.

Now isn't ideal. They're stressed. I don't want to pile on. I'll bring it up later.

Sometimes, that restraint is wise.

But other times, it's fear dressed up as patience.

The truth is, there will almost never be a moment where clarity feels perfectly comfortable. If you wait for emotional ease, you'll wait indefinitely.

What matters more than perfect timing is anchored delivery.

Clarity doesn't require bluntness.
It doesn't require confrontation.
It requires being grounded.

Avoiding clarity in the name of timing doesn't preserve peace, it postpones honesty.

And postponed honesty tends to surface later under pressure.

There's also an unseen cost to waiting emotional labor.

When you're unclear, you have to remember what you didn't say. You have to manage expectations you never corrected. You have to manage misunderstandings you helped create.

Clarity reduces emotional labor because it removes guesswork.

Once expectations are named, you don't have to keep managing them internally.

I didn't realize how much energy I was spending maintaining vagueness until I stopped doing it. Conversations became shorter. Follow-ups decreased. Resentment softened, not because people always agreed with me, but because they weren't confused about where I stood.

Clarity simplified my life.

How Backwards Thinking Distorts Clarity

Backwards thinking shows up here too.

Instead of asking, what needs to be said clearly? We ask, how will this be received?

Instead of anchoring in truth, we anchor in reaction.

When reaction becomes the reference point, clarity gets filtered. Words are adjusted to manage outcomes rather than express reality. And while that might feel considerate, it often creates confusion instead.

People don't need you to predict their reaction. They need you to be honest about your position.

Clarity doesn't guarantee agreement.
It guarantees understanding.

And understanding is the foundation of trust.

One belief that kept me avoiding clarity was the idea that being clear was selfish.

If I say this clearly, it might inconvenience them. If I draw this boundary, it might disappoint them. If I state what I need, it might feel demanding.

But clarity isn't selfish when it's honest.
It's only selfish when it's careless.

Avoiding clarity to protect feelings often protects your discomfort more than their well-being.

When Clarity Strengthens Relationships

Here's the part that surprised me the most: clarity doesn't weaken healthy relationships, it strengthens them.

When clarity is expressed calmly and respectfully:

- Expectations become realistic
- Resentment decreases

- Communication simplifies
- Emotional labor is reduced

People may not always like what you say, but they respect knowing where you stand.

And respect lasts longer than approval.

Clarity matters most in relationships that continue.

With strangers, the uncertainty may fade. With coworkers, friends, spouses, and family, it compounds.

Unspoken expectations don't disappear, they turn into assumptions. Unstated boundaries don't dissolve, they get crossed. Unclear communication doesn't stay neutral, it creates narratives.

Clarity resets the story.

It says, this is where I stand now. Not forever. Not immovably. But honestly.

Saying the Hard Thing Simply

Clarity doesn't require emotional dumping.

It doesn't mean saying everything you feel. It means saying what actually belongs.

Clarity sounds like:

- "I'm not comfortable with that."
- "That doesn't work for me."
- "I need more time."
- "I want to be honest with you."

These statements are grounded. They don't attack. They don't over-explain.

They simply state reality.

And reality, when stated calmly, gives people something solid to respond to.

Clarity also becomes easier with practice.

Say no when the consequence is small. State preferences when it doesn't feel urgent. Name boundaries before they're violated.

Clarity becomes less risky when it becomes familiar.

Why This Chapter Matters

This chapter exists because clarity was one of the hardest disciplines for me to practice, not because I lacked words, but because I cared deeply about impact.

I had to learn that caring about impact doesn't mean avoiding truth.

It means delivering truth with intention.

Clarity isn't reckless.
It's responsible.

And while it may feel risky in the moment, it prevents far greater damage later.

The Emotional Cost of Avoiding Clarity

Avoiding clarity doesn't just affect conversations, it affects you.

It creates mental loops. Rehearsed explanations. Imagined outcomes. Unsent messages you keep refining in your head.

You relive conversations that haven't happened yet. You anticipate reactions you haven't received. You manage emotional outcomes that aren't even real.

That internal noise has a cost.

I noticed that when I avoided clarity, I carried conversations longer than necessary. Days later, I was still thinking about what I should have said. Weeks later, I was still adjusting my behavior to accommodate something that could have been resolved with one clear statement.

Clarity would have been uncomfortable for a moment.
But avoidance made it exhausting over time.

That's the trade-off most people don't calculate.

Silence feels cheaper up front.
Clarity feels expensive up front.
But silence charges interest.

It drains energy.
It erodes confidence.
It quietly teaches you that your needs are negotiable, even when they aren't.

Over time, avoiding clarity doesn't just weaken communication. It weakens self-trust. You start questioning your instincts. You hesitate longer. You second-guess what you already know.

And once you lose trust in your own clarity, conversations become harder, not easier.

That's why this chapter matters.

Not because clarity is polite.
But because clarity is stabilizing.

When You Finally Choose Clarity

What finally pushed me toward clarity wasn't confidence, it was fatigue.

I got tired of replaying conversations in my head. Tired of adjusting my behavior around things that had never been said. Tired of carrying responsibility for other people's assumptions.

Clarity stopped feeling like a risk when avoidance started feeling heavier.

I realized that every time I stayed unclear, I was still choosing an outcome, I just wasn't choosing it intentionally. I was choosing confusion. I was choosing emotional labor. I was choosing to manage consequences later instead of addressing reality now.

Clarity didn't suddenly make conversations easy.
But it made them honest.

And honesty simplified things.

Even when clarity led to discomfort, the discomfort had an edge, it moved. It resolved. It didn't linger the way unspoken tension does.

That's when I understood this:

Clarity doesn't remove risk.
It removes confusion.

And confusion is far more damaging over time than any honest conversation could ever be.

Application Layer, Chapter Nine

Before your next difficult conversation, ask:

- What am I avoiding saying clearly?
- What truth feels risky to name?
- What am I hoping will resolve itself?

Then ask:

- Can I say this calmly?
- Can I say this simply?
- Can I say this without apology or aggression?

Clarity isn't reckless.
It's responsible.

Anchoring Scripture

"Speaking the truth in love, we are to grow up in every way."

Ephesians 4:15

Reflection Prompts, Chapter Nine

1. Where do I hesitate most to be clear?
2. Am I willing to go through emotional labor at the expense of being clear?
3. How has delayed clarity affected my relationships?
4. What would change if I trusted clarity more?
5. Who might benefit if I spoke more plainly?

Opportunity, Chapter Nine

Clarity creates alignment.

Alignment reduces tension.
Reduced tension builds trust.
Trust strengthens connection.

Clarity may feel risky.
Misalignment is far more costly.

When you speak clearly, you give others something real to respond to.That's where real communication begins.

Chapter Ten

When Silence Speaks Louder Than Words

"There is a time to be silent and a time to speak."

Ecclesiastes 3:7

Wisdom is knowing the difference

There was a time I believed that silence was neutral.

Not good. Not bad. Just empty space between words.

If something mattered, you talked about it. If something didn't, you stayed quiet. Silence, in my mind, was simply what happened when there was nothing left to say, or nothing worth saying yet.

I was wrong.

Silence is never empty.
It always communicates something.

The question is whether it communicates what you intend, or something you never meant to say at all.

Over time, I began to notice that some of the most impactful moments in my life weren't shaped by words, but by absence of words. Conversations that never happened. Pauses that lingered too long. Moments where clarity was available but left untouched in the name of peace, restraint, or timing.

Silence doesn't just sit there.

It fills the room.

And whatever fills the room shapes the relationship.

The Myth of "Saying Nothing"

One of the most dangerous assumptions we make is believing that silence equals non-participation.

As if choosing not to speak means choosing not to affect the situation.

But silence is a position.

When you don't speak, you still communicate:

- Acceptance
- Avoidance
- Disapproval
- Fear
- Distance
- Or restraint

The problem is this: you don't get to decide which one of these they hear unless the silence is understood and anchored.

I've learned this the hard way.

There were moments when I stayed quiet because I thought I was being wise. I didn't want to escalate things. I didn't want to say something I'd regret. I didn't want to make a situation heavier than it already was.

But me being silent wasn't always me using wisdom.

It read as withdrawal.

Other times, my silence read as agreement when I didn't agree at all. Or as indifference when I was actually overwhelmed. Or as calm when internally I was anything but.

Silence spoke for me, and it said the wrong thing.

When Silence Feels Safer Than Words

Silence often feels safer than speech because it delays consequence.

Words commit you. Silence postpones commitment.

If you speak, you might disappoint someone. If you stay quiet, you can still adjust later. If you speak, you reveal where you stand. If you stay quiet, you preserve flexibility.

That flexibility feels protective.

But protection through silence comes at a cost.

Unspoken clarity doesn't disappear, it turns into tension. And tension doesn't stay hidden forever. It leaks into tone. Into distance. Into conversations that feel heavier than they should without anyone knowing why.

Silence doesn't preserve peace.
Unexamined silence quietly erodes trust.

The Difference Between Disciplined Silence and Avoidant Silence

This distinction changed everything for me.

Not all silence is the same.

Disciplined silence is intentional. Avoidant silence is reactive.

Disciplined silence sounds like:

- I'm not ready to respond yet.
- I need time to think before I speak.
- This moment doesn't require words.

Avoidant silence sounds like:

- I hope this goes away.
- I don't want to deal with the reaction.
- If I stay quiet, I won't make it worse.

One creates space.
The other creates distance.

The challenge is that both look identical from the outside.

Only intention separates them.

And if you don't clarify your intention, someone else will eventually assign one to you.

How Backwards Thinking Uses Silence as a Shield

Backwards thinking doesn't always show up as over-talking.

Sometimes it hides behind quiet.

Instead of anchoring in truth and choosing whether silence serves the moment, backwards thinking asks:

- What's the least risky move right now?
- How do I avoid friction?
- How do I stay in control without engaging?

Silence becomes a shield instead of a strategy.

It feels responsible. It feels mature. It feels contained.

But it often creates confusion instead of clarity.

People don't know where they stand with you. They don't know what you're thinking. They don't know whether your silence means safety, or distance.

And uncertainty invites interpretation.

The Emotional Weight of Unspoken Words

What surprised me most was how heavy silence became over time.

It wasn't peaceful. It was exhausting.

I replayed conversations in my head, not because of what was said, but because of what I didn't say. The boundary I softened. The truth I delayed. The honesty I didn't speak only hurt me and my partner in the end.

Silence created mental noise.

That noise followed me into future conversations, making me guarded, cautious, and internally braced. I wasn't entering conversations freely, I was entering them already carrying what I hadn't said before.

Words may be risky. But unspoken words carry weight too.

And that weight accumulates.

When Silence Becomes Leadership

Here's the other side of the truth: silence can be powerful.

Not the silence of avoidance, but the silence of someone who is settled.

There are moments when silence:

- Prevents escalation
- Allows others to process
- Signals confidence instead of insecurity
- Creates room for reflection

This kind of silence isn't empty.

It's anchored.

Anchored silence doesn't come from fear.
It comes from regulation.

You're not quiet because you're unsure. You're quiet because you're intentional.

That kind of silence feels different to everyone in the room.

It doesn't confuse. It steadies.

Learning to Name Silence When Necessary

One of the most practical shifts I've made is learning to name my silence.

Instead of disappearing into it, I clarify it.

Statements like:

- "I'm quiet because I want to think before responding."
- "I'm not avoiding this, I just need time."
- "I hear you. I'm processing."

Those words protect silence from being misinterpreted.

They keep silence from doing damage it was never meant to do.

Silence doesn't need to be filled.
But sometimes it needs to be explained.

Silence in Close Relationships

Silence hits differently depending on context.

In marriage. In parenting. In leadership. In friendship.

The closer the relationship, the heavier silence becomes.

In close relationships, silence often feels personal, even when it isn't intended that way. What might feel like restraint to one person can feel like withdrawal to another.

I had to learn that silence requires more care, not less, the closer the relationship is.

Silence without reassurance can create insecurity. Silence without clarity can feel like distance. Silence without context can feel like rejection.

When trust is involved, silence must be paired with presence.

When Silence Turns Into Control

This was one of the hardest truths for me to face.

Sometimes silence isn't humility. It's control.

By staying quiet, I avoided vulnerability. I avoided reaction. I avoided accountability.

Silence allowed me to stay protected while the other person sat in uncertainty.

That wasn't discipline. That was self-preservation.

And self-preservation disguised as restraint still damages connection.

True discipline doesn't protect you at someone else's expense.

What Silence Reveals About You

Just like listening, silence reveals who you are.

It shows:

- How comfortable you are with tension
- How secure you are in your position
- How willing you are to let moments breathe
- How afraid you are of consequence

Silence exposes your relationship with discomfort.

And discomfort is where growth happens.

When Silence Teaches People How to Treat You

One of the quiet realities I had to confront is this: silence doesn't just communicate how you feel, it teaches people what you will tolerate.

When you stay silent repeatedly around the same behavior, pattern, or dynamic, others don't experience that as neutrality. They experience it as permission. Not always intentional permission, but permission, nonetheless.

I didn't realize how often my silence trained people unintentionally.

I thought I was being patient. I thought I was being gracious. I thought I was choosing my battles wisely.

But over time, my silence became a message:
This is acceptable.
This doesn’t need to change.
This doesn’t require acknowledgment.

And when I finally did speak, weeks, months, or years later, it felt sudden to them. Out of character. Overdue in my mind, but surprising in theirs.

That disconnect wasn’t their fault.

I had taught them what silence meant.

Silence, when repeated, becomes precedent.

And precedent shapes expectation.

That realization forced me to take responsibility not just for what I said, but for what I consistently didn’t.

Silence vs. Stillness

Another distinction that changed how I think about communication is the difference between silence and stillness.

Silence is external. Stillness is internal.

You can be silent and internally frantic. You can be still and barely speaking at all.

Stillness is regulated presence. Silence without stillness is restraint under pressure.

I had practiced silence for years without learning stillness. I knew how to hold my tongue, but I didn’t know how to settle my body. My breathing was shallow. My posture was tight. My mind was rehearsing responses instead of resting in the moment.

People can feel that.

Silence without stillness feels tense. Silence with stillness feels grounded.

That's why two people can say nothing, and one feels safe while the other feels distant.

The difference isn't volume. It's regulation.

When you're still internally, silence communicates confidence. When you're unsettled internally, silence communicates withdrawal.

Learning stillness gave silence a different texture. It softened it. It stabilized it. It made it usable.

When Silence Is the Last Honest Option

There are moments when silence isn't avoidance, it's integrity.

When words would escalate rather than clarify. When emotion hasn't settled enough to speak cleanly. When anything you say would be premature.

In those moments, silence isn't weakness.
It's wisdom.

But here's the key: those moments are temporary.

Silence can be the right move now without becoming the permanent move forever.

The danger isn't silence itself.
It's silence with no intention to return to clarity.

Silence should create space, not erase responsibility.

When silence is chosen wisely, it buys you time.
When silence is chosen habitually, it costs you trust.

Why This Chapter Matters

This chapter exists because silence shaped many of my relationships more than I realized.

Not because I was cold. Not because I was careless. But because I underestimated silence's power.

Silence isn't absence.
It's communication without words.

When used intentionally, it strengthens relationships. When used carelessly, it quietly weakens them.

When Silence Protects You From Yourself

One final truth I had to accept is this: sometimes silence isn't about protecting the relationship, it's about protecting my own ego.

There were moments when speaking clearly would have forced me to take responsibility sooner than I wanted. Moments when clarity would have exposed inconsistency in my actions, not just tension in the relationship. Silence allowed me to delay that reckoning.

As long as I didn't say anything, I could keep my internal narrative intact. As long as I stayed quiet, I didn't have to adjust my behavior. As long as clarity was postponed, accountability was too.

That was uncomfortable to admit.

Silence can feel virtuous when it's actually evasive. It can look like patience when it's really self-protection. And until I acknowledged that dynamic honestly, silence kept serving me more than it served the relationship.

True discipline meant asking a harder question:
Am I being quiet to preserve peace, or to preserve comfort?

Once I started answering that question honestly, silence stopped being a default. It became a decision. And decisions carry responsibility.

Application Layer, Chapter Ten

Before your next meaningful pause, ask:

- What am I protecting with this silence?
- Is this silence serving clarity, or avoiding it?
- Does this moment require space, or reassurance?

If silence is chosen, anchor it.
If silence is reactive, address it.

Silence should never do your communicating for you.

Anchoring Scripture

"There is a time to be silent and a time to speak."

Ecclesiastes 3:7

Reflection Prompts, Chapter Ten

1. When does silence feel safest for me?
2. Where has my silence been misunderstood?
3. How do I typically use silence under pressure?
4. What relationships need clearer communication around silence?
5. What would intentional silence look like in my life?

Opportunity, Chapter Ten

Silence, when anchored, becomes strength.

It slows conversations.
It steadies emotions.
It protects clarity.

You don't need to speak more.
You need to silence with intention.

That's how presence becomes powerful.

Chapter Eleven

The Blind Spots We Don't See Coming

"Search me, O God, and know my heart,

test me and know my anxious thoughts."

Psalm 139:23

Blind spots shrink when we invite inspection.

If backwards thinking and backwards talking had one defining trait, it would be this:

They rarely feel wrong while they're happening.

They don't announce themselves as mistakes. They don't arrive with raised voices or obvious conflict. Most of the time they feel reasonable, even responsible. They feel like you're trying to do the right thing.

That's what makes them dangerous.

The most damaging communication patterns in our lives aren't usually the ones we recognize immediately. They're the ones we operate from without realizing it. The habits that feel normal. The reactions that feel justified. The internal pace we've grown used to and stopped questioning.

Those are blind spots.

And the costliest blind spots aren't the ones we don't know exist.

They're the ones we sense, but don't want to look at.

Why Blind Spots Are So Hard to Detect

Blind spots survive because they don't feel like gaps. They feel like instincts.

You don't experience them as errors. You experience them as judgment calls. As timing decisions. As communication style. As "this is just how I process things."

Backwards thinking doesn't feel backwards because it often sounds logical. It presents itself as clarity, decisiveness, or honesty. It moves fast, but it feels purposeful.

It sounds like:

- "I need to respond now before this goes sideways."
- "If I don't clarify this immediately, it'll get worse."
- "I'm just being direct."
- "I'm just trying to prevent misunderstanding."

And because those thoughts feel responsible, we trust them.

But the moment we trust unexamined urgency; we stop leading the conversation and start reacting to it.

That's where the blind spot forms, not in what we say, but in what we don't notice before we speak.

How Backwards Thinking Creates Blind Spots

Backwards thinking is the most common blind spot because it happens before language.

It's the internal sequencing error where:

- emotion outruns clarity
- urgency replaces intention
- reaction precedes anchoring

When thinking moves faster than awareness, the mind fills gaps automatically. Assumptions form. Interpretations harden. Conclusions arrive early.

And because this process happens internally, it feels invisible.

You don't experience it as backwards. You experience it as efficient.

Backwards thinking convinces you that speed is responsibility, that response equals leadership, and that silence is risk. It creates blind spots not by hiding information, but by reordering it incorrectly.

That's why blind spots feel justified. They're powered by thinking that never slowed down long enough to be examined.

Familiarity Is a Powerful Blindfold

Blind spots persist because they're familiar.

You're used to your internal pace.
Used to how tension feels in your body.
Used to jumping in quickly.
Used to explaining.
Used to defending.
Used to managing outcomes instead of anchoring direction.

Familiarity creates comfort, even when it creates damage.

Just because something feels natural doesn't mean it's aligned.

Just because it's habitual doesn't mean it's healthy.

Backwards talking often sounds calm.
Often sounds thoughtful.
Often sounds controlled.

That's why it survives scrutiny.

It doesn't feel like chaos. It feels like competence.

And competence, when it goes unexamined, becomes dangerous.

When Awareness Begins to Narrow

This is where the work deepens.

Once awareness increases, the field narrows. You start noticing things you missed before, not because they weren't there, but because you were moving too fast to see them.

You start noticing:

- how quickly your body reacts before your mind settles
- how silence triggers urgency
- how often you interrupt, not with words, but with posture or tone
- how explanation shows up before understanding

These moments aren't failures.

They're signals.

Blind spots don't disappear through effort. They disappear through awareness.

And awareness doesn't shout.

It whispers.

The Blind Spots We Protect

Some blind spots are accidental.

Others are defended.

We protect them because they've helped us survive. Because they've worked before. Because they've given us a sense of control, safety, or belonging. Because they've helped us avoid discomfort.

We defend them by labeling them:

- "my personality"
- "how I communicate"
- "being honest"
- "just being real"

But defense is always a signal.

The more quickly we justify a pattern, the less likely we are to examine it.

Backwards thinking thrives inside justification.

We don't just repeat the behavior, we explain why it's necessary. We don't just ignore feedback, we reinterpret it. We don't just miss the blind spot, we protect it.

That's when patterns harden.

Warning Signs You're Inside One

This chapter is a warning because blind spots leave evidence.

They show up as:

- the same conversations repeating with different people
- explanations getting longer instead of clearer
- tension that feels familiar rather than surprising
- relationships that feel heavier without a clear reason
- moments where you're "right," but disconnected

When the same breakdown keeps happening, it's rarely coincidence.

It's usually unexamined thinking replaying itself.

Backwards talking doesn't always explode. Sometimes it erodes.

And erosion is harder to see, until something collapses.

When Blind Spots Become Backwards Talking

Backwards talking is what blind spots sound like.

It's not yelling. It's not chaos. It's language that arrives out of sequence.

You speak before anchoring. You explain before understanding. You clarify before listening. You defend before being challenged.

And because the words themselves may be accurate, the damage isn't obvious.

Backwards talking often sounds calm.
Often sounds thoughtful.
Often sounds controlled.

But it carries the weight of unexamined thinking.

That's why people respond to tone instead of content. That's why conversations drift instead of resolve. That's why intentions don't come through.

Blind spots don't just distort what you say,
they distort when you say it.

And timing, more than wording, determines impact.

Heightened Awareness Changes Responsibility

Once you see a pattern, responsibility shifts.

You don't get to unknow what you've noticed. You don't get to keep calling reaction "communication." You don't get to hide behind intention alone.

Heightened awareness doesn't demand perfection. It demands ownership.

Ownership looks like:

- catching yourself earlier
- slowing down sooner
- choosing restraint before explanation
- pausing when urgency rises

This isn't about becoming silent.
It's about becoming intentional.

Discipline begins when awareness stops being optional.

When Blind Spots Feel Threatening

Awareness can feel uncomfortable at first.

Because blind spots protect us from seeing where we're misaligned. When they're exposed, the instinct is often to defend instead of reflecting.

We feel challenged. We feel misunderstood. We feel tempted to explain rather than examine.

That reaction is human.

But it's also revealing.

The discomfort isn't coming from being wrong. It's coming from losing certainty.

And certainty, when it's unexamined, is often just familiarity.

Why This Chapter Sits Exactly Here

This chapter is intentionally placed.

The reader needs awareness. Without awareness, nothing will change. Awareness of the problem makes you responsible to it.

They need to recognize that most communication damage isn't malicious, it's mechanical, that the danger isn't what we say, it's what we never stop to question.

Once blind spots are visible, movement changes.

You don't rush the same way. You don't speak the same way. You don't react the same way.

Because awareness alters posture.

This Is a Warning, and an Invitation

This chapter is not about shame.
It's about preparation.

It's an invitation to slow down before something gets said that can't be unsaid. To notice the internal moment before words, form. To recognize that most breakdowns are predictable once patterns are visible.

Blind spots don't make us weak.
Refusing to see them does.

The Cost of Refusing Awareness

Unacknowledged blind spots don't stay neutral.

They create:

- repeated misunderstandings
- emotional fatigue
- quiet resentment
- unnecessary conflict

And over time, they shape identity.

You don't just communicate this way. You become someone people brace for.

That's not because you're unkind. It's because you're unexamined.

Awareness interrupts that trajectory.

Application Layer, Chapter Eleven

For the next week, don't fix anything.

Just notice.

Notice:

- when urgency rises
- when silence feels threatening
- when explanation replaces curiosity
- when your body reacts before your words

Write it down if you can.

Awareness always precedes change.

Anchoring Scripture

"Search me, O God, and know my heart,

test me and know my anxious thoughts."

Psalm 139:23

Reflection Prompts, Chapter Eleven

1. What communication patterns in my life feel familiar, but unresolved?
2. Where do I feel most justified in my reactions?
3. What feedback have I dismissed because it felt uncomfortable?
4. How do I usually respond when my thinking is challenged?
5. What might change if I treated awareness as leadership?

Opportunity, Chapter Eleven

When awareness increases:

- reactions lose power
- conversations slow down
- clarity becomes possible

This chapter isn't about fixing.
It's about seeing.

Because once you see what's loaded, you don't move the same way.

Chapter Twelve

The Fifteen Guns

"The wisdom from above is first pure, then peaceable, gentle, open to reason."

James 3:17

Wisdom does not arrive armed.

It arrives anchored.

For a long time, I thought the problem in difficult conversations was what I said.

I assumed that if things went sideways, it must have been my wording, my timing, or my tone. Maybe I spoke too quickly. Maybe I didn't explain myself clearly enough. Maybe I chose the wrong moment.

What I didn't see was what I was carrying into the conversation before I ever opened my mouth.

I wasn't walking into conversations empty-handed.

I was walking in armed.

Not visibly. Not aggressively. But internally, I was carrying what I've come to think of as fifteen guns, layers of protection, bracing, and self-defense that had nothing to do with the other person and everything to do with how unsafe I felt being fully present.

The problem wasn't that I was hostile.

The problem was that I was prepared for conflict in moments that only required clarity.

And when you bring fifteen guns into a conversation, everything changes, even if you never fire a single one.

What "The Fifteen Guns" Actually Means

This metaphor isn't about violence. It's about posture.

The fifteen guns represent the internal arsenal we carry into conversations when we are braced instead of anchored. They are the explanations lined up before we're questioned. The defenses rehearsed before we're accused. The exits identified before we've even entered the room.

They are not loud. They are not obvious. They are not intentional. They are protective instincts that we learned, somewhere along the way, that conversations were not always safe.

And protection, when it leads, always reshapes communication.

You can be calm. You can be articulate. You can sound reasonable. And still be armed.

That's what made this so difficult for me to see.

The Fifteen Guns We Carry

I didn't realize how many weapons I carried until I started noticing how often I wasn't actually listening.

Here are the guns I learned I brought into conversations, sometimes all at once. But sometimes I carried two, sometimes six, but I was always carrying.

1. The Explanation Gun

Prepared just in case I'm misunderstood.

This shows up as over-clarifying too early. Talking before the other person finishes. Explaining intent instead of receiving impact.

Backwards thinking says: I need to make sure they understand me.
Backwards talking explains something that hasn't even been questioned yet.

2. The Defense Gun

Ready in case blame appears.

Even neutral statements feel like accusations when this gun is loaded. Tone sharpens. And the wall of protection always shows up with the Defense Gun. Even though it's not needed.

Defense rarely waits for an attack, it anticipates one.

3. The Justification Gun

Loaded to prove I'm reasonable.

This gun turns conversations into case studies. Evidence replaces presence. Logic replaces listening.

It sounds calm. It feels mature. It shuts people down quietly.

4. The Control Gun

Aimed at managing the direction.

This shows up as steering, redirecting, reframing, or prematurely resolving. It's not dominance, it's anxiety disguised as leadership.

5. The Timing Gun

Used to delay clarity.

Now isn't the right moment. Let's talk later. This isn't productive.

Sometimes that's wisdom. Often, it's fear.

6. The Image Gun

Protects how I'm perceived.

This gun edits truth to make it easier to swallow. Softens what needs firmness. Waters down clarity to preserve approval.

7. The Urgency Gun

Fires when discomfort rises.

Talking speeds up. Silence feels dangerous. The need to "fix" replaces the ability to stay.

Urgency feels responsible.
It's usually panic.

8. The Withdrawal Gun

Activated when engagement feels risky.

Silence becomes distance. Presence fades. Not to punish, but to self-protect.

This gun says nothing, but it still wounds.

9. The Counterpoint Gun

Prepared before listening finishes.

Rebuttals form mid-sentence. You're still hearing words, but meaning is already lost.

10. The Outcome Gun

Fixated on resolution.

This gun rushes toward closure before understanding. It values ending the conversation over honoring it.

11. The Boundary Gun (Misused)

Set too early or too sharply.

Healthy boundaries are anchored. This version is reactionary, built to stop discomfort, not define truth.

12. The Minimization Gun

Downplays impact to reduce tension.

It's not that big of a deal.
You're reading too much into it.

This gun erodes trust slowly.

13. The Authority Gun

Speaks from position instead of presence.

Titles. Experience. Seniority. Logic.

Used to end discussion instead of deepening it.

14. The Emotional Mask Gun

Appears calm but is rigid.

No anger. No volume. Just immovability.

Calm without flexibility is still armor.

15. The Silence Gun

The most dangerous one.

Silence that punishes. Silence that withholds. Silence that communicates distance instead of presence.

Silence can be wisdom, or weaponry.

How Backwards Thinking Arms Us

Backwards thinking doesn't start with words.

It starts with bracing.

It sounds like:

- I need to be ready in case this turns.
- I should explain now before this goes wrong.
- I don't want this to escalate.
- I can't lose control of this moment.

Those thoughts feel responsible. They feel mature. They feel wise.

They are usually fear.

And fear, when it leads, arms you.

Once armed, you are no longer fully present. You're scanning instead of receiving. Preparing instead of understanding. Managing instead of connecting.

That's when backwards talking shows up, not as aggression, but as premature action.

Words arrive too soon. Tone sharpens. Listening shortens.

The conversation fractures, not because of what was said, but because of what was being carried.

When Protection Replaces Presence

What shocked me most was realizing how often my protection cost connection.

I thought I was keeping conversations safe. I thought I was preventing conflict. I thought I was being careful.

But people could feel it.

They felt managed. They felt rushed. They felt like I was already somewhere else.

Fifteen guns don't make a conversation safer.

They make it tense.

Even if no one can name why.

Lowering the Guns in Real Time

Lowering the guns doesn't mean becoming passive.

It means becoming anchored.

It looks like:

- Letting someone finish even when you feel misunderstood
- Pausing instead of clarifying immediately
- Allowing silence without filling it
- Trusting that understanding doesn't need urgency

Anchored thinking disarms you internally before you speak externally.

And when the guns are down, something changes.

Your body relaxes. Your tone softens. Your words come out cleaner.

Not because you said less, but because you stopped protecting what didn't need defending.

What It Feels Like When the Guns Are Still Up

One of the hardest parts of lowering the guns is that you don't always feel armed when you are.

There were conversations where I genuinely believed I was calm, present, and open, until the moment passed and something didn't sit right. The words were fine. The tone was controlled. Nothing "went wrong."

And yet, connection didn't deepen.

That's when I started noticing more subtle signs.

My body would lean forward slightly, not in interest, but in anticipation. My breathing would stay shallow. My mind would track the conversation instead of resting in it.

I wasn't aggressive. I wasn't defensive. But I was prepared.

Prepared to correct. Prepared to explain. Prepared to redirect if things drifted somewhere uncomfortable.

That preparation didn't make me dangerous, but it made me unavailable.

The other person could feel it, even if neither of us could name it. The conversation stayed polite. Productive, even. But it never fully relaxed.

That's the quiet cost of carrying guns you never fire.

The Moment You Realize You're Armed

For me, the realization usually comes too late.

It shows up after the conversation ends, when I replay it and realize how often I was one sentence ahead. How I anticipated pushback that never came. How I answered questions that weren't asked.

That's when I recognize it.

I wasn't listening to understand. I was listening to stay ahead.

And staying ahead is another form of control.

Not malicious. Not manipulative. Just protective.

The guns come up fastest in moments that matter most, when clarity feels risky, when emotion is present, when something important is on the line. That's when the old instinct says, Be ready. Don't get caught off guard.

But presence requires the opposite posture.

It requires you to risk being caught in the moment.

Why Lowering the Guns Feels Unsafe at First

Lowering the guns feels unsafe because it removes the illusion of control.

When you stop preparing your response while the other person is still talking, you don't know exactly where the conversation is going. When you stop explaining yourself early, you don't know how your words will land. When you stop managing outcomes, you have to tolerate uncertainty.

That discomfort is real.

Especially if you've learned, over years or decades, that conversations can turn quickly, that misunderstanding can escalate, that being unprepared has consequences.

Lowering the guns doesn't mean those experiences didn't happen. It means they no longer get to run the room.

Anchored thinking doesn't erase history. It keeps history from hijacking the present.

The First Few Times You Try This

The first few times you enter a conversation unarmed, it feels awkward.

You pause longer than you normally would. Silence stretches. Your body wants to jump in.

Everything in you says, Do something.

And instead, you stay.

You listen longer. You breathe. You let the other person finish, even when you're sure you know where they're headed.

And something unexpected happens.

The conversation doesn't collapse. You don't lose ground. You aren't misunderstood beyond repair.

In fact, most of the time, the moment softens.

Not dramatically.
Quietly.

That quiet shift is the sound of trust forming.

What Changes When You Keep the Guns Down

Over time, something else changes too.

You stop feeling exhausted after conversations. You replay them less. You feel less need to revisit, clarify, or repair.

Not because everything goes perfectly, but because you weren't fighting internally the whole time.

When the guns are down:

- Your words arrive slower, but come out cleaner
- Your tone stays open instead of guarded
- Your presence feels supportive instead of strategic

People don't brace when you speak. They don't rush to defend themselves. They stay in the conversation longer.

That's when communication stops feeling like work and starts feeling like alignment.

The Discipline This Chapter Is Really About

This chapter isn't about eliminating instinct.

It's about discipline before reaction.

The discipline to notice when you're armed. The discipline to lower what you're carrying. The discipline to trust presence more than preparation.

That discipline doesn't make conversations easy. It makes them honest.

And honesty, when it's anchored, doesn't destroy connection. It deepens it.

Why This Chapter Matters

This chapter exists because I didn't need better language.

I needed fewer weapons.

Most of the conversations I regret didn't go wrong because I was angry or careless. They went wrong because I was armed when I didn't need to be.

Presence requires vulnerability. Vulnerability requires safety. Safety begins internally.

When you lower the guns, you don't lose power.

You gain clarity. Now you are able to plant good seeds and water those seeds when you go into conversations unarmed. Unarmed conversations require vulnerability. And being vulnerable is real power.

Application Layer, Chapter Twelve

Before your next meaningful conversation, ask yourself:

- Which gun am I carrying right now?
- What am I preparing to defend?
- What outcome am I trying to control?

Then ask:

- What would it look like to enter this moment unarmed?
- What if I trusted presence more than protection?

Lowering the guns doesn't make you weak.

It makes you available. It makes you vulnerable and that's when real human connection begins.

Anchoring Scripture

"The wisdom from above is first pure, then peaceable, gentle, open to reason."

James 3:17

Reflection Prompts, Chapter Twelve

1. Which of the fifteen guns do I carry most often?
2. How does bracing show up in my body before I speak?
3. What am I afraid will happen if I don't protect myself?
4. Where has protection cost me connection?
5. What conversations in my life would change if I entered unarmed?

Opportunity, Chapter Twelve

When you lower the guns:

- Listening deepens
- Tension softens
- Conversations slow down in the right way

You don't have to win the moment. You don't have to manage the outcome.

You just have to be present.
That's where the guns finally go down.

Chapter Thirteen

The Blind Spots You Don't Feel

"Therefore, let anyone who thinks that he stands take heed lest he fall."

1 Corinthians 10:12

Awareness without humility is unstable

This isn't the blind spot from before. That one hides in what you haven't noticed yet. This one hides in what you're already proud of noticing.

One of the most dangerous moments in personal growth isn't when you're unaware.

It's when you believe you're aware enough.

By the time someone reaches this point, after learning about anchored thinking, emotional discipline, listening, clarity, and even threat awareness, it's easy to assume the hardest work is behind them. You know the language now. You recognize the patterns. You can spot backwards talking when it happens. You understand why conversations derail. You've slowed down. You've learned to pause. You've learned not to jump in as fast as you used to.

And that's exactly why this chapter matters.

Because awareness, by itself, can create a new blind spot.

Not the obvious kind. Not the loud kind. The quiet kind. The kind that doesn't announce itself. The kind that feels like confidence.

The worst blind spots aren't the ones we don't know about. They're the ones we stop checking for.

When Awareness Becomes Assumption

There's a subtle shift that happens once you start "doing the work."

You pause more. You interrupt less. You listen longer. You regulate better.

And over time, a quiet narrative can creep in:

I'm not doing that anymore. I've grown past that. That used to be me.

The problem is that growth doesn't eliminate patterns. It just makes them quieter.

Backwards thinking doesn't disappear when you recognize it. It adapts.

Instead of obvious interruptions, it shows up as:

- calculated silence
- controlled restraint
- internal judgment
- selective listening
- subtle impatience masked as calm

You're no longer reacting impulsively. But you may still be reacting internally.

And internal reactions shape conversations just as much as spoken ones.

This is where many people get stuck without realizing it. They assume that because they aren't doing the old thing, they must be doing the right thing. But awareness without continued anchoring slowly turns into assumption. And assumption is one of the most dangerous forms of backwards thinking.

The Blind Spot of "I'm Being Careful"

One of the most convincing blind spots is caution.

It sounds responsible. It feels mature. It looks disciplined.

But sometimes, being careful is just backwards thinking with better posture.

You're quiet, but not open. You're calm, but already decided. You're listening, but filtering.

You're no longer rushing to speak. Instead, you're silently steering the moment. You're deciding internally which parts matter and which don't. You're choosing when to engage based on comfort rather than curiosity.

This is where backwards thinking evolves.

It no longer feels frantic. It no longer feels defensive. It feels reasonable.

And that's what makes it dangerous.

Because when you stop checking your internal posture, conversations begin drifting again, just more subtly than before.

Awareness Without Re-Anchoring Drifts

Awareness isn't a destination. It's a condition that requires maintenance.

The moment you stop re-anchoring; you begin operating on assumption.

You assume:

- your tone is coming across well
- your silence feels supportive
- your restraint feels safe
- your clarity is understood

But assumption is just another form of backwards thinking.

It moves the reference point from the moment itself to your interpretation of the moment.

And perception, unchecked, lies. And the truth is in the awareness of both perspectives. But getting to that truth is the obstacle.

This is where people start missing things again, not because they don't care, but because they believe they already see clearly. They stop asking, what's happening right now? And start relying on what usually happens.

This chapter exists to slow you back down.

Not because you're doing it wrong, but because this is where people drift without noticing.

The Quiet Return of Backwards Thinking

Backwards thinking rarely announces itself at this stage.

It shows up as:

- I already know where this is going

- I've heard this before
- This doesn't need as much space
- I can see the pattern here

And maybe you can.

But the moment you stop allowing space, you stop allowing truth to fully emerge.

Listening turns selective. Presence turns performative. Discipline turns rigid.

And rigidity always creates distance.

The danger here isn't explosion. It's erosion.

How Blind Spots Show Up in Everyday Life

One of the hardest things to accept about blind spots is that they don't show up when things are going badly.

They show up when things feel fine.

At home, this looks like thinking you're being patient while your spouse feels unheard. You're calm. You're composed. You're not interrupting. But internally, you've already decided what the issue is, and that decision quietly shapes how you listen.

At work, it looks like believing you're being efficient while someone else feels dismissed. You think you're streamlining the conversation. You think you're helping move things forward. But what you're actually doing is skipping over context that mattered to them.

In leadership, it looks like confidence turning into certainty. You've seen this pattern before. You've handled this type of situation before. So instead of staying curious, you stay comfortable. And comfort slowly replaces attentiveness.

None of these moments feel dramatic.

That's why they're dangerous.

They don't trigger alarms. They don't feel emotional. They don't feel reactive.

They feel controlled.

And control, unchecked, is often just backwards thinking in disguise.

When Good Intentions Become a Blind Spot

One of the most difficult blind spots to confront is the belief that good intentions automatically equal good impact.

You care. You're trying. You've learned. You've grown.

And because of that, it's easy to assume that if something goes wrong, the issue must be external.

But blind spots don't come from a lack of care. They come from unexamined certainty.

Backwards thinking at this stage sounds like:

- I'm trying to help
- I'm being calm
- I'm not reacting
- I'm doing what I've learned

All of those things can be true, and still miss the moment.

Because backwards thinking isn't always loud anymore. Sometimes it's quiet confidence that no longer checks itself.

And when thinking drifts backward, talking eventually follows.

You explain instead of clarifying. You respond instead of receiving. You manage instead of engaging.

And before you realize it, you're once again working from the end of the conversation backward, trying to fix impact instead of anchoring intention.

The Inside-Out Check That Prevents Drift

This is where everything in this book comes back to one central truth:

Communication is an inside-out job.

Blind spots form the moment you stop checking yourself and start monitoring the room instead.

You read reactions instead of your posture. You manage outcomes instead of your internal state. You focus on being "right" internally instead of being present relationally.

Anchored thinking requires returning inward before responding outward.

It asks:

- Am I rushing internally even if I look calm?
- Am I listening to confirm what I believe?
- Am I protecting my position instead of the relationship?
- Am I assuming alignment instead of verifying it?

Those questions don't mean you're failing. They mean you're still practicing.

And practice is the difference between discipline and drift.

Why This Chapter Is a Guardrail

This chapter exists because this is where most people quietly plateau.

Not because they stop caring. Not because they regress. But because they stop re-checking.

They know enough to feel confident. They've learned enough to feel settled. And slowly, that groundedness hardens.

This chapter is the guardrail that keeps growth from turning into rigidity.

It reminds you that:

- Anchoring is ongoing
- Listening must remain curious
- Discipline must stay flexible
- Awareness must stay humble

Because the blind spots you don't feel are the ones that cost the most over time.

Conversations don't fall apart. They flatten.

They lose depth. They lose honesty. They lose the sense that someone is actually being received.

When You Stop Feeling the Slip

Earlier in the book, backwards talking felt obvious.

You could feel it in your body. In your urgency. In your defensiveness.

Here, it feels different.

You don't feel rushed. You don't feel reactive. You don't feel anxious.

You feel… controlled.

And control feels safe, until it isn't.

Because control doesn't invite honesty. It invites caution.

People sense it, even if they can't articulate it. They begin to simplify what they share. They avoid edges. They stop offering the full picture.

Not because you're unsafe, but because you're not fully open.

That's one of the most dangerous blind spots there is.

A Subtle Example You Might Recognize

There have been moments where I thought I was doing everything right.

I wasn't interrupting. I wasn't defensive. I wasn't raising my voice.

But internally, I had already decided what mattered.

I was listening, but only for confirmation. I was present, but not receptive. I was calm, but closed.

Nothing "went wrong" in those conversations. No explosion. No argument. But something didn't move either. The conversation ended flatter than it started. The connection didn't deepen. And later, I would realize that while I hadn't said the wrong thing, I hadn't been as open as I thought.

That's the blind spot you don't feel.

You don't feel anxious. You don't feel threatened. You feel composed.

And yet, you've subtly removed yourself from the exchange.

Heightened Awareness Requires Humility

This chapter is a warning, but a compassionate one.

The more skilled you become in communication, the easier it is to forget that discipline must remain flexible.

True anchoring isn't stiffness. It's responsiveness.

It allows you to:

- adjust mid-conversation
- soften when needed
- stay curious even when you "know"
- let someone finish even when you're confident

Backwards thinking returns the moment certainty replaces curiosity.

And certainty feels good. That's why it's dangerous.

The Discipline of Re-Checking Yourself

This chapter re-anchors one simple question:

What's happening in me right now?

Not:

- What should I say?
- How should I respond?
- How do I manage this?

But:

- Am I open?
- Am I settled?
- Am I listening to understand, or to confirm?

The most mature communicators don't assume they're aligned. They check.

They don't trust silence alone. They trust presence.

They don't assume silence means they're calm. They keep checking themselves.

How This Protects You From Backwards Talking

At this stage, backwards talking doesn't sound like chaos.
It sounds like explanation.
Like correction.
Like quiet dismissal.

It shows up after the conversation, when you realize:

- you responded to part, not the whole
- you filled gaps instead of asking
- you assumed meaning instead of confirming it

And once again, you're working backwards, explaining what you meant instead of anchoring what you said.

That's why this chapter matters.

It prevents the return of backwards talking by keeping backwards thinking visible, even when it feels "disciplined."

Why This Chapter Exists

This chapter isn't here to teach a new skill.

It's here to protect the ones you've already learned.

Because growth doesn't fail loudly. It fails quietly, when vigilance fades.

This is the chapter that says:

Don't stop paying attention.
Don't assume you've arrived.
Don't let awareness harden into identity.

Anchoring is a practice. Listening is a posture. Discipline is dynamic.

And backwards thinking is patient.

It waits for confidence.

Application Layer, Chapter Thirteen

Periodically ask yourself:

- What am I assuming right now?
- Where might I be listening selectively?
- Am I open, or merely controlled?
- Have I stopped checking because I feel "past this"?

Re-anchoring isn't regression.
It's leadership.

Anchoring Scripture

"Therefore, let anyone who thinks that he stands take heed lest he fall."

1 Corinthians 10:12

Reflection Prompts, Chapter Thirteen

1. Where have I grown confident enough to stop checking myself?
2. What blind spots might exist because I feel disciplined?
3. How does my silence feel to others?
4. Where might certainty be limiting curiosity?
5. What does re-anchoring look like for me right now?

Opportunity, Chapter Thirteen

This chapter gives you something rare:

A chance to stay grounded after growth.

Not sharper.
Not louder.
Not more advanced.

Just more grounded.

Because the strongest communicators aren't the ones who know the most,
they're the ones who keep paying attention.

Chapter Fourteen

When Pressure Reveals the Pattern

"Better a patient person than a warrior,

one with self-control than one who takes a city."

Proverbs 16:32

Strength under pressure is restraint

Pressure doesn't create new habits. It reveals existing ones.

That's something I didn't understand for a long time.

I thought the reason conversations went wrong under stress was because the moment itself was difficult. High stakes. Fatigue. Emotion. Timing. I told myself that if the pressure wasn't there, the conversation would have gone differently.

But pressure wasn't the cause.

It was the amplifier.

Under pressure, you don't rise to your best intentions. You default to your strongest patterns.

And for me, those patterns often included backwards thinking, followed quickly by backwards talking.

Why Things Fall Apart When They Matter Most

Most people communicate "well enough" when life is calm.

Low stakes. Plenty of time. No emotional weight. No fear of loss.

But real life doesn't live there.

Real conversations happen:

- when you're tired
- when you feel misunderstood
- when something important is on the line
- when emotions are already present
- when the outcome matters

That's when pressure enters.

And pressure has a way of stripping away polish.

It compresses time. It heightens sensitivity. It narrows perception.

Suddenly, you're not just talking, you're protecting, defending, bracing, preparing.

And that's where backwards thinking sneaks back in.

Not loudly. Not obviously. But efficiently.

Backwards Thinking Under Pressure

Under pressure, backwards thinking doesn't sound chaotic.

It sounds urgent.

It sounds like:

- "I need to explain this before it gets worse."
- "If I don't say something now, I'll lose ground."
- "They're misunderstanding me."
- "I can't let this be received incorrectly again."

Those thoughts feel responsible. They feel proactive. They feel necessary.

But they're still backwards.

Because the reference point quietly shifts.

Instead of anchoring in clarity, presence, and understanding,
you anchor in reaction management.

You stop asking:
What's actually happening here?

And start asking:
How do I control where this goes?

That shift is subtle. But it changes everything.

Pressure Narrows the Lens

One of the most dangerous things pressure does is narrow your focus.

You stop seeing the whole moment.
You zoom in on:

- one sentence
- one tone
- one word
- one perceived threat

And once your focus narrows, your responses follow.

You begin responding to parts instead of the whole. You answer before the picture is complete. You react to what you think is being said, not what is being said.

That's how conversations derail even when no one intended them to.

Not because people are careless, but because pressure collapses perspective.

The Illusion of "Handling It Well"

Here's the part that took me a long time to admit.

Some of my worst conversations didn't look bad on the surface.

I didn't raise my voice. I didn't explode. I didn't say anything overtly cruel.

I stayed composed.

But I wasn't solid.

I was managing myself just enough to appear calm, while still letting urgency drive my words.

That's a dangerous place to be.

Because when you look controlled, people assume alignment. But when you feel unsettled, your words still carry tension.

Tone tightens. Timing shifts. Presence hardens.

And people feel it, even if they can't name it.

When Calm Is Performing Instead of Grounded

There were moments where I honestly thought I had grown.

I wasn’t loud. I wasn’t reactive. I wasn’t escalating the situation.

And because of that, I assumed I was doing better.

But looking back, I can see the difference now.

I wasn’t anchored. I was managing perception.

My calmness wasn’t coming from being grounded, it was coming from effort. I was holding myself together instead of settling myself. And that distinction matters more than most people realize.

Because effort eventually leaks.

Even when words are composed, people feel tension when calm is forced. They sense when someone is monitoring themselves instead of being present. And that kind of calm doesn’t relax a conversation, it constricts it.

I’ve learned that pressure exposes this faster than anything else.

When I’m truly anchored, calm feels spacious.
When I’m performing calm, everything feels narrow.

I become careful. I choose words defensively. I hold my posture instead of relaxing into it.

Nothing is technically “wrong,” but nothing fully opens either.

That's when conversations stall without conflict. That's when people stop offering their full thoughts. That's when things feel unfinished without anyone knowing why.

And the hardest part is this: from the inside, it still feels like progress.

That's the blind spot pressure reveals.

Because pressure doesn't just test how you speak, it tests why you're speaking the way you are.

Am I staying calm to stay connected?
Or am I staying calm to stay in control?

Those two things look similar on the outside. They feel very different on the inside. And they lead to very different outcomes.

True groundedness doesn't feel tight.
It feels available.

It allows space. It invites completion. It lets the other person finish, even when it's uncomfortable.

Performance tries to protect. Anchoring tries to understand.

And pressure always exposes which one you're relying on.

Pressure Exposes What You Haven't Anchored

Pressure doesn't invent weaknesses. It exposes unanchored areas.

If your thinking isn't anchored, pressure speeds it up.
If your listening isn't anchored, pressure makes it selective.
If your clarity isn't anchored, pressure makes it defensive.
If your discipline isn't anchored, pressure makes it rigid.

That's why so many people say, "I don't know why I said it that way."

You didn't choose it. Pressure did.

Because anchoring wasn't in place before the moment arrived.

The Moment That Decides the Direction

There is always a moment, small, quiet, internal, where direction is decided.

It's not the sentence you say. It's the moment before the sentence.

That split second when:

- your body tightens
- your thoughts accelerate
- your need to be understood rises
- your fear of being misread shows up

That moment decides whether the conversation stabilizes or slips.

Most people miss it.

They think the problem starts with words.

It doesn't.

It starts with posture.

Anchoring Inside the Pressure

Anchoring under pressure doesn't mean eliminating emotion.

It means managing your direction while emotion is present.

That looks like:

- slowing your response even when urgency is screaming
- letting the other person finish even when you feel threatened
- choosing precision over speed
- choosing clarity over control

Anchoring here is not passive. It's disciplined.

It's saying:
"I don't need to win this moment to protect myself."
"I don't need to explain yet."
"I don't need to react right now."

That restraint changes outcomes.

When Pressure Tempts You to Over-Explain

One of the most common pressure responses is explanation.

Not thoughtful explanation. Defensive explanation.

The kind that shows up when you feel misunderstood.

You say one thing. It goes wrong. And suddenly, you're talking backwards trying to fix the impact instead of owning the process.

Explanation piles up. Tone shifts. Intent gets buried. And the more you explain, the less grounded you sound.

That's not because explanation is wrong.

It's because timing matters.

Explanation before understanding feels like justification. Explanation before listening feels like dismissal. Explanation before anchoring feels like panic.

Pressure Doesn't Need a Performance

One of the quiet lessons this chapter carries is this:

Pressure doesn't require brilliance. It requires being grounded.

You don't need the perfect words.
You don't need to solve the moment.

You just need to stay present.

Presence keeps the conversation alive. Performance shuts it down.

Under pressure, people don't listen for intelligence. They listen for safety.

And safety comes from self-management.

Staying Human Under Pressure

This chapter matters because pressure is unavoidable.

Marriage. Parenting. Leadership. Work. Conflict. Loss. Fatigue.

You will not always be rested. You will not always be calm. You will not always feel clear.

That doesn't disqualify you.

What matters is whether you can:

- notice pressure without obeying it
- feel emotion without letting it steer
- slow yourself down even when the moment is fast

That's maturity.

Why This Chapter Exists

This chapter exists because this is where everything is tested.

Not in theory.
Not in reflection.
Not in hindsight.

But in real time.

When pressure enters the room, it asks one question:

What actually leads you right now?

If it's urgency, the conversation speeds up.
If it's fear, the conversation tightens.
If it's control, the conversation hardens.

But if it's anchored thinking,
the conversation steadies.

One thing pressure does exceptionally well is remove your script.

It strips away rehearsed responses. It collapses prepared explanations. It exposes whether your calm is real, or rehearsed.

When pressure rises, you don't rise to the occasion. You fall back to what's been practiced.

If anchoring hasn't been practiced, pressure reveals control. If listening hasn't been practiced, pressure reveals urgency. If discipline hasn't been practiced, pressure reveals justification.

That's why pressure often feels unfair.

You can care deeply. You can intend well. You can believe you're doing the work.

And still discover, under pressure, that you've been leaning on effort instead of grounding.

This isn't failure. It's feedback.

Pressure isn't here to embarrass you. It's here to show you where practice needs to deepen.

Because once anchoring is internal, pressure no longer exposes weakness.

It exposes leadership.

Application Layer, Chapter Fourteen

When pressure shows up, pause long enough to ask:

- What am I feeling in my body right now?
- Am I reacting to a threat, or responding to reality?
- Do I need to speak now, or do I need to stay present?
- Is this urgency helping, or hijacking me?

Pressure doesn't require immediate answers.
It requires grounded presence.

Anchoring Scripture

"Better a patient person than a warrior,

one with self-control than one who takes a city."

Proverbs 16:32

Reflection Prompts, Chapter Fourteen

1. How does pressure usually change my communication?
2. Where do I feel urgency rise fastest?
3. What does my body do before my words derail?
4. When have I mistaken composure for being truly grounded?
5. What would anchoring look like for me under pressure?

Opportunity, Chapter Fourteen

Pressure will come. The question isn't whether you'll feel it, it's whether you'll let it lead.

When anchored thinking leads:

- conversations stay intact
- trust survives tension
- clarity arrives without force

Pressure doesn't have to break communication.

It can reveal maturity.

Chapter Fifteen

The Moment You Choose to Stay Present

"Be still, and know that I am

God."

Presence isn't passive. It's the decision to remain grounded when movement would be easier

There's a quiet moment that comes near the end of any real change.

It isn't loud. It isn't dramatic. It doesn't announce itself as growth.

It feels ordinary.

That's the moment most people miss.

Because by the time you reach it, you already know the language. You've learned about anchored thinking. You've seen how backwards thinking leads to backwards talking. You've practiced listening. You've slowed down. You've caught yourself mid-sentence. You've noticed your tone. Your posture. Your urgency.

And now, life resumes.

Conversations still happen. Stress still shows up. People still misunderstand you. You still misunderstand others.

The difference isn't that conflict disappears.

The difference is that you notice yourself sooner.

That's what this chapter is about.

Not mastery. Not perfection. Not a final technique.

It's about the moment you realize you have a choice, and you take it.

The Choice, You Didn't Know You Had Before

Earlier in this book, backwards talking felt inevitable.

You felt it in your chest. Your posture tensed up. In your need to explain. In your impulse to jump in.

It happened fast.

So fast you didn't realize you were already reacting until the words were out.

Now, something subtle has changed.

There's a fraction of a second, sometimes barely noticeable, where you feel the old urge rise… and you don't move yet.

That pause is everything.

That pause is where the entire book lives.

Because in that moment, you’re no longer a passenger to your thinking. You’re present with it.

You notice:

- the urge to defend
- the desire to be understood immediately
- the anxiety of silence
- the temptation to steer the conversation

And instead of obeying it automatically, you stay.

This is where most people think they’ve arrived.

They haven’t.

This is where the real work begins.

Why Most People Revert Here

This stage is dangerous because it feels stable.

You’re no longer blowing things up. You’re no longer obviously reactive. You’re no longer saying things you instantly regret.

So, you relax.

And when vigilance relaxes, backwards thinking changes shape.

It doesn’t come back as chaos.

It comes back as:

- confidence
- certainty
- quiet control
- subtle correction
- “I already know where this is going”

You're not interrupting, you're waiting to redirect. You're not reacting, you're internally bracing. You're not rushing, you're deciding ahead of time.

Outwardly, you look calm.

Internally, you've already moved.

That's why the final discipline isn't about slowing down.

It's about staying open longer than feels necessary.

Small Talk for Smart People, Revisited

By now, you understand this book was never about surface conversation.

"Small talk" was never the point.

It was always about small moments:

- the first five seconds of a response
- the breath before you speak
- the silence you don't fill
- the tone you choose instead of justifying
- the pause you allow instead of rushing

Smart people don't dominate conversations. They don't perform clarity. They don't weaponize intelligence.

They stay present.

Presence is what gives small moments weight.

And weight is what makes communication matter.

Backwards Thinking, One Last Time

Backwards thinking never disappears.

It waits.

It waits for:

- fatigue
- familiarity
- certainty
- comfort
- confidence

It whispers:
"I've done this already."
"I know this pattern."
"I don't need to slow down here."
"This doesn't require the same care."

That's when it gets you.

Not through loud mistakes, but through quiet shortcuts.

Backwards talking doesn't always sound wrong. Sometimes it sounds polished. Sometimes it sounds calm. Sometimes it sounds reasonable.

But it still misses.

Because it isn't anchored in this moment.
It's anchored in what you expect next.

The discipline you're choosing now is simple, but not easy:

Stay where you are.
Listen longer than feels efficient.
Let the other person finish fully.
Resist the urge to wrap it up before it's ready.

That's not passivity.

That's leadership.

What It Looks Like When This Is Working

When you live this way consistently, something unexpected happens.

You speak less, and connect more.
You explain less, and are understood more.
You argue less, and resolve more.
You feel calmer, not because things are easier, but because you're more grounded.

People start finishing their thoughts around you. Tension de-escalates faster. Misunderstandings surface sooner, before damage sets in.

Not because you control conversations , but because you no longer rush them.

This is the quiet power of presence.

The Cost of Not Choosing It

Here's the truth most books avoid:

You can read everything in this book and still revert.

Not because you failed,
but because presence requires choice every time.

There is no autopilot. There is no permanent setting. There is only awareness, renewed repeatedly.

If you stop choosing it:

- urgency returns
- tone sharpens
- explanations lengthen
- defensiveness creeps back
- conversations flatten again

Not dramatically. Gradually.

That's why this chapter exists.

Not to teach you something new , but to remind you where to stand.

Where You Are Now

If you're here, you already know this:

You haven't mastered anything. You've noticed something.

And noticing is the beginning of everything.

You've noticed how quickly things go sideways.
You've noticed how often clarity is rushed.
You've noticed how silence feels threatening.
You've noticed how much power there is in waiting.

That awareness doesn't make you better than anyone else.

It makes you responsible.

Responsible for how you enter moments. Responsible for how you stay present. Responsible for when you speak, and when you don't.

That's not pressure.

That's ownership.

This Is Where It Becomes a Way of Living

If there's one thing I hope you take from this book, it isn't a method.

It's a posture.

Because the work you've been doing isn't about learning how to talk better.

It's about learning how to be better before you talk.

That's the part most people skip.

They want language. They want scripts. They want strategies.

But communication doesn't break down because people lack words. It breaks down because people lose themselves in the moment.

They rush. They brace. They protect. They perform.

And then they wonder why conversations feel exhausting.

Presence fixes what performance never will.

You Will Be Tested, Quietly

The test won't come in dramatic confrontations.

It will come in:

- casual disagreements
- tired evenings
- familiar relationships
- people you assume "should know you by now"
- moments where you feel justified

That's where backwards thinking returns.

Not loudly. Not obviously.

It returns as entitlement.

"I shouldn't have to slow down here."
"They know what I mean."

"I don't need to explain this carefully."
"This isn't that serious."

Those thoughts feel harmless.

They're not.

They're the doorway back to old patterns.

And the difference now is this:

You'll feel it sooner.

That tightening. That leaning forward. That urge to clarify before listening. That need to make your point.

That's your signal.

Not to speak.
But to stay.

Staying Is the Discipline

Staying doesn't mean agreeing. It doesn't mean surrendering truth. It doesn't mean shrinking.

It means not abandoning yourself, or the other person, in the moment.

It means:

- letting silence do its work
- letting emotion settle before directing it
- letting the conversation finish forming
- letting understanding come before response

Staying is how you keep conversations human.

And humanity is what makes communication effective.

Why This Was Never About Being Right

You may have noticed something as you read.

This book doesn't reward cleverness. It doesn't celebrate verbal dominance. It doesn't glorify "winning" conversations.

Because being right has never been the goal.

Alignment is.

You can be right and still miss someone. You can be right and still damage trust. You can be right and still be unsafe to talk to.

But when you're anchored , when your thinking is anchored , your words don't need force.

They are received because they belong.

That's the difference.

Communication is the foundation of every relationship. Not just what is said–but how you approach the moment itself. Because conversation was never meant to be transactional. It was built to be relational.

Without that, we wouldn't need each other at all. We just exist side by side–talking, but never truly connecting.

A be-by-myself-ship instead of a relationship.

Every interaction creates something, whether you realize it or not.
Memories work like movies of the mind.

And the moments inside them–the small exchanges,
the tone, the timing–those are the commercials that interrupt the story.

Short scenes that still shape how the whole thing is remembered.

The question isn't whether you were creating moments. You are.

The question is what kind. How many moments have you stolen? How many have you given?

Do people enjoy coming to talk to you – or do you just enjoy talking?

Because in every interaction, you're choosing. Not someday. Not down the road.

Right now.

You're either a "Moment Taker", or a "Moment Giver."
A "Moment Thief", or a "Moment Saint."

And that choice doesn't start with words. It starts with thinking.

Small Talk, One Final Time

Small talk for smart people was never about sounding smart.

It was about thinking clearly in small moments.

Moments where:

- tone matters
- posture matters
- timing matters
- restraint matters
- presence matters

Smart people don't rush those moments.

They respect them.

Because they understand something most people don't:

Small moments decide big outcomes.

Anchoring Scripture

"Be still, and know that I am

God."

A Note to the Reader

If you're still reading, I want to speak to you directly.

Not as an author.
Not as an expert.
Not as someone who has this figured out.

But as someone learning in real time, just like you.

I didn't write this because I mastered communication.
I wrote it because I kept seeing where I missed it.

At home.
At work.
In leadership.
In relationships that mattered too much to keep getting wrong.

I've said things backwards.
I've rushed clarity.
I've defended when I should've listened.
I've explained when I should've paused.
I've spoken too quickly and repaired too late.

And I'm still learning.

This book isn't a declaration.
It's a confession.

A record of what I'm noticing.
What I'm correcting.
What I'm choosing differently, one conversation at a time.

If you see yourself in these pages, that doesn't mean you're broken.

It means you're paying attention.

And attention changes everything.

What I Hope You Carry Forward

I hope you don't carry language that creates distance.
I hope you don't carry techniques.
I hope you don't carry pressure to "do this right."

I hope you carry awareness.

Awareness of:

- when you're rushing
- when you're bracing
- when you're reacting
- when you're assuming
- when you're no longer present

And when you notice it, even late, I hope you pause instead of panic.

Progress isn't measured by never slipping.

It's measured by how quickly you return.

The Final Invitation

You don't need to announce that you've changed.
You don't need to explain your growth.
You don't need to prove anything.

Just stay present.

Listen longer.

Speak slower.
Choose clarity over urgency.
Choose presence over reaction.
Choose understanding before response.

Do that consistently, imperfectly, and conversations will change.

Not because you're smarter.
But because you're anchored.

And anchored people don't talk backwards.

They speak from where they are.

Final Reflection

Before your next conversation, ask yourself:

Am I here?
Am I settled?
Am I listening to understand?
Am I choosing presence over performance?

That's it.

That's the work.

Closing Thought

Backwards thinking leads to backwards talking.

But anchored thinking leads to conversations that last. Conversations that last equal lasting relationships.

And the moment you choose to stay present ,

that's the moment everything changes.

At the end of the day, nothing in this book works without choice.

You can understand every concept and still walk into moments unprepared. You can recognize your patterns and still repeat them. Awareness alone doesn't change conversations, presence does.

Staying present doesn't mean you'll always get it right. It means you stopped defaulting to who you've been when pressure shows up. It means you slow your thinking before you speak. It means you decide, again and again, not to steal moments that were never yours to take.

Every conversation gives you a chance to lead differently.

Not perfectly. Not flawlessly. But honestly.

And when you choose to stay present, something shifts.

The moment softens.

The person in front of you feels it.

And the story you're creating, whether you realize it or not, changes direction.

That choice is always yours.

And it always starts right now.

Note from the Author

If you're holding this book at the end, I want you to know something first:

I didn't write this because I had it all figured out.

I wrote it because I didn't.

This book came out of real conversations, many of them unfinished, some of them painful, and a few that surprised me in the best way. It came out of moments where I spoke too quickly, listened too narrowly, or entered a conversation already braced instead of present. It came out of learning, sometimes the hard way, that good intentions don't matter as much as anchored thinking.

Especially with the people you love most.

At home.
In marriage.
With children.
At work.
In leadership.

I've learned that conversations don't usually fall apart because people don't care. They fall apart because people are moving too fast internally. Because anxiety gets ahead of clarity. Because the need to be heard overtakes the discipline to listen. Because backwards thinking quietly turns into backwards talking before we even realize it's happening.

I've lived that.

And I'm still learning my way through it.

This book wasn't written to make you better at talking.

It was written to help you become more aware while you're talking.

Aware of when you rush.

Aware of when you're already preparing a response.

Aware of when silence feels uncomfortable instead of intentional.

Aware of when your body, tone, or timing is saying more than your words ever could.

If there's one thing I hope you carry with you after reading this, it's not a technique.

It's a pause.

A moment where you notice what's happening inside you before you speak.

A moment where you let someone finish, not just their sentence, but their thought.

A moment where clarity replaces urgency.

Because when that happens, conversations change, not dramatically, but meaningfully.

I don't expect this book to fix every conversation in your life.

I don't expect you to get it right every time.

I don't get it right every time either.

But if this book helped you slow down even once…

If it helped one conversation reach someone differently…

If it helped you feel more grounded, more present, or more aware in moments that used to derail…

Then it did what it was meant to do.

"And we know that in all things God works for the good of those who love him, who have been called according to his purpose."
— Romans 8:28

Every conversation you've had, the ones that went sideways, the ones you wish you could take back, the ones where you finally got it right, none of it was wasted. God was working in all of it. Including this one.

Thank you for reading.
Thank you for reflecting.
And thank you for choosing to pay attention, to yourself, and to the people in front of you.

— Shawn

Anchor Points

This is one line per chapter, not a summary, just where I still catch myself. I'm not past any of these. This is what I'm still checking for, chapter by chapter.

Chapter One — Anchored Thinking Comes First

I still forget to check myself before I speak. When I skip it, my words end up doing the checking for me.
And they never do it gently.

Chapter Two — The Illusion of Being Resolution-Based

I still want to fix things before I've actually heard them.
I'm learning to ask what they need from me right now. Not rush toward an answer.

Chapter Three — Listening Isn't Passive—It's Most Powerful

I still catch myself forming my response before someone's finished talking.
Counting to three before I answer is still a discipline. Not a habit. Not yet.

Chapter Four — Emotional Discipline Creates Credibility

I still let emotion lead sometimes, before I even notice it's happening.
Naming what I'm feeling before I speak is the one thing that slows it back down.

Chapter Five — Timing Is Everything

I still confuse urgency with importance more than I'd like to admit.
I'm learning to ask whether something needs to be said now, or said well.

Chapter Six — Why Timing Matters More Than Truth

I still want to say the true thing the moment I see it.
I'm learning that waiting for it to be received isn't avoidance.
It's stewardship.

Chapter Seven — When Words Are Used as Weapons (Even Quietly)

I still notice, after the fact, when my words were built to shut something down instead of open it up.
I'm working on trading statements for invitations.

Chapter Eight — When Clarity Feels Like Conflict

I still pad the truth when I'm afraid of how it'll be received.
I'm learning to ask whether I'm anchored, or just trying to control what happens next.

Chapter Nine — When Clarity Feels Risky

I still soften things I should just say plainly.
I'm learning to ask what I'm avoiding. And whether I can say it without apology or defensiveness.

Chapter Ten — When Silence Speaks Louder Than Words

I still use silence to protect myself more often than I want to admit.
I'm learning to ask whether it's chosen. Or just reaction, wearing a calm face.

Chapter Eleven — The Blind Spots We Don't See Coming

I still try to fix things before I've actually noticed them.
Some weeks, the only discipline I can manage is just paying attention.

Chapter Twelve — The Fifteen Guns

I still walk into hard conversations carrying more than I need.
I'm learning to ask which gun I'm holding. And what it would take to set it down.

Chapter Thirteen — The Blind Spots You Don't Feel

I still mistake feeling calm for actually being open.
I have to keep re-checking, even now. Because re-anchoring isn't regression. It's the work.

Chapter Fourteen — When Pressure Reveals the Pattern

I still find out what I'm made of under pressure. And it's not always who I want to be.
Pressure doesn't need an immediate answer from me. Just an anchored one.

Chapter Fifteen — The Moment You Choose to Stay Present

I still feel the old urge rise, in the pause before I speak. Staying there a little longer than feels comfortable is still the whole book. Every time.

What Comes Next

This book was about what came out of my mouth. The backwards thinking. The backwards talking. The small moments I kept missing, without even realizing it.

The next one is about who kept showing me where it came from.

My wife, Stephanie, has been both my mirror and my anchor, since before I had language for either.

The next book is about what it costs to actually look at your reflection. Instead of just standing near it.

That one isn't finished yet.

This one had to come first.

Where This Goes From Here

If this book stayed with you, there's more waiting.

Becoming a Moment Giver isn't a switch you flip once and forget. It's a practice.

That's why the next step isn't another chapter. It's reflection notes, built to help you walk through real conversations as they happen.
For those of us still in the middle of the climb, so we can walk through it together.

There's more coming beyond that too. Keynotes. Workshops. A companion app called Genesis of Me.

Not everything is built yet.
But it's coming.

For updates, visit risefivellc.com. Or reach out directly at risefivellc@gmail.com.

www.ingramcontent.com/pod-product-compliance
Lightning Source LLC
Chambersburg PA
CBHW021418260726
48782CB00053B/287

* 9 7 9 8 2 3 4 0 1 5 6 4 8 *